"education is the key to unlock the golden door of freedom"

—george washington carver

How to Write a College Application Essay

*expert advice to help you
get into the college of your dreams*

t a n i a   r u n y a n

:FG *field guide series*

 T. S. Poetry Press • New York

T. S. Poetry Press
Ossining, New York
Tspoetry.com

© 2017, 1st Edition, by Tania Runyan

This book includes various references from or to the following companies, brands, and sources: Playtex, Playtex Products LLC; Lady Lee; McCormick & Company; Volvo, The Volvo Group; Skype, a division of Microsoft; *To Kill a Mockingbird* by Harper Lee, J.P. Lippincott & Co. (1960); AP and SAT, divisions of The College Board; ACT; Adidas; *Family Matters*, ABC; "Material Girl" by Madonna, *Like A Virgin*, Sire Records (1984); *The New Yorker*; The Common Application; Coalition for Access, Affordability & Success; Walgreens; Purdue Online Writing Lab, https://owl.english.purdue.edu/owl/; *The Hunger Games* by Suzanne Collins, Scholastic (2008); *Brave New World* by Aldous Huxley, Chatto and Windus (1932); Saving Tiny Hearts Foundation; "Letter From Birmingham Jail" by Martin Luther King, Jr. (1963); *Black Boy* by Richard Wright, Harper and Brothers (1945); *Bluest Eye* by Toni Morrison, Holt, Rinehart & Winston (1970); *Autobiography of Malcolm X* by Malcolm X, Grove Press (1965); Ben and Jerry's Phish Food, a trademark of Unilever; Post-it, a trademark of 3M; Steinway & Sons; Shedd Aquarium; Kumon North America; "Don't Stop Believing" by Journey, *Escape*, Columbia (1981); The Super Bowl, NFL; "Rolling in the Deep" by Adele, 21, XL/Columbia (2010); Lokeswarananda Eye Foundation; Rush Medical Center; Public Allies; Greystone.

Cover image by L.L. Barkat

ISBN 978-1-943120-16-1

Library of Congress Cataloging-in-Publication Data:
Runyan, Tania
    [Nonfiction/Writing.]
    How to Write a College Application Essay:
      Expert Advice to Help You Get Into the
      College of Your Dreams, 1st Edition
    ISBN 978-1-943120-16-1
    Library of Congress Control Number: 2017934530

for my past students, who in finding their voices
have helped me find my own

—tania runyan

Contents

An Introduction

I've guided thousands of students and parents over the years who believe the college application essay is just another *form* amidst the dizzying pile of paperwork (or digital fields) that must be filled out, submitted, and quantified.

Without a doubt, you've amassed a lot of data over your high school years: grades, test scores, and activity lists. But the application essay? That's your time to shine, to truly be you. To—get ready for this—**have fun.**

In this guide, we'll be exploring what the college application essay is all about. Why do you have to write it? What kind of writing is it? When and how should you start? What can you learn about writing—and yourself—through this milestone process?

Meanwhile, the best way to prepare as a college-bound student—or a teacher of one—is to get a taste for excellent short-form autobiographical writing (often called "flash" nonfiction or "shorts"). Still months or years away from your senior year? You can start this part of the application process at any time. It's never too early to get inspired by good prose!

A Simple Start

Read and savor the following short autobiographical essays. These pieces were written by published authors, not college applicants, and demonstrate the key qualities of narrative writing that you'll be developing in your personal statements. Imagine the settings, voices, actions, and people. Go where the writers take your senses. "Feel all the feels"—sadness, humor, frustration, embarrassment—of the narrators as you prepare to express yourself in a way that will make schools want to nab you. What will make them desire to get to know you better over the next four years? For starters, good prose.

~

Canning Tomatoes
by Cathy Warner

My mother and I crouch in a tomato field off Road 98, pulling and twisting red globes from thick hairy stalks, gently setting them into generic black yard bags that we heft down the rows, bumping against our bare calves, which are yellow from the tomatoes' pollen sweat and the pesticide powder that pours in vapor trails from the belly of the crop dusters early in the season.

It's late August in the Sacramento Valley and the automatic harvesting machine manned by its crew of migrant workers will roll through this field tomorrow. Today, the farmer and his wife—parents of my high school friend—have invited my freshly-divorced mother and me to pick our fill.

So, like post-biblical gleaners in the growing heat, we fill our plastic bags with thick-skinned canning tomatoes and load them into the back of my mother's Pinto until, wiping the sweat from our faces with the backs of our sticky yellowed garden gloves, my mother decides we've picked enough. I wince as I sit on the hot vinyl car seat, my dusty thighs burning. My mother starts the car and we thump down the dirt access alongside an irrigation ditch toward the asphalt road, the windows open, the dust and tang of hot tomatoes filling our nostrils.

At home, wearing yellow Playtex gloves, we wash, blanch, and peel the scalding tomatoes from their skins. We drop them into canning jars, sprinkle in salt, set on lids, twist on rings, and set the lidded jars in the water bath until they've steamed themselves sealed. In years past, my mother has cooked with Lady Lee canned tomatoes. This year, she bought a canning kettle and jars. An investment for future use, since there is no alimony from this, her second, dissolved marriage, and her new job—medical receptionist at a clinic where another high school friend's father is a doctor who hired my mother, who had no experience in the field—pays just above minimum wage.

Together my mother and I put up dozens of jars of tomatoes, and during the coming year, she will turn each into either spaghetti sauce or enchilada sauce with a dash of McCormick's seasoning. Biting into the tomatoes we canned ourselves, wiping their residue from our mouths, we feel proud of our efforts. Through the fall, winter, and spring eating the rich sauce folded into pasta and tortillas dilutes the taste of our new poverty, our need for charity, until summer comes and we find ourselves in the blistering heat, kneeling in the farmer's field, picking his tomatoes once again.

A Loss for Words

by Aaron Housholder

The OR buzzed with activity: nurses set up the baby's station, orderlies stacked supplies in back, technicians monitored machines that went "ping!" My wife lay still in the center of it all. She smiled at me. Her surgical cap matched the half-curtain that blocked the view of the rest of her body. The doctor on the other side of the curtain wore gloves to her elbow, a face shield, a soldier's look in her eyes. She had been here with us before. She was cutting, I supposed, but I (mercifully) couldn't see for sure. I kissed my wife and sat to her right, as directed.

The practiced casualness of the room struck me. The technicians and surgical nurses joked with us, saying things like, "We're gonna get this baby out soon" and "This little girl seems to have a mind of her own." But their laughter felt forced. We found out later that this same surgical team had performed our emergency C-section the year before, the night we lost Benjie. They hoped now with all their collective might to make this delivery successful. They sought redemption.

All at once our doctor's steady cutting quickened. Her sudden urgency snapped the room into silence, rendered all words profane. The doctor pulled and tugged with such violence that it seemed impossible she was working with my wife's living flesh. For several minutes, everyone in the room bowed forward under the weight of exquisite, expectant stillness. I closed my eyes.

With the first gurgling cry the room itself seemed to exhale and then explode. Livie's voice rechristened the space for words. My wife said, "She's crying," her voice thick with her own tears. A nurse ran out to the waiting room and told our family, "She's screaming!" meaning, yes, the baby's alive. She had to tell them several times, the words too heavy to hold all at once. I put my lips to my wife's forehead, a long quiet kiss.

I found myself moments later with surgical shears in my hand as our nurse Kara offered to let me cut the cord. I had not planned to do it—I had not cut the cord with our first child Scottie—but in the bliss of that particular moment, I whispered, "Yes, please."

And then someone said, "Would you like to hold her now?"

I only nodded. My words were smothered again.

Door

by Lauren Melissa

I let yesterday pass quietly. Not the actual day, but the significance. I didn't mention it to anyone. I didn't dwell on it. I did what I could to make it mine.

Yesterday was full of cleaning and errands. I tackled everything that I could in the span of the day. I wasn't trying to prove anything. There wasn't anything special happening. It just felt like a good day to start over.

Today flat out came for my life. Not my real life, my emotional one. Today brought the kind of frustration that leads to throwing things in the front yard. The neighbors know that it happens from time to time, but the people who were at the church across the street stayed for the show. The frustration mounted into a solid angry cry. The tears burned my already hot and sweaty cheeks as they poured off of my face and onto the shower floor. The melodies of Train and the roar of the water drowned out my pitiful sobs.

Today was a reminder that I am fallible. It was humbling. It sat me down. It pissed me off. It reminded me that no matter how hard I work and how much effort I put in, the results aren't always what I expect. Will it work out? Absolutely. Did I learn that I am capable of more than I think sometimes? Yes. Can I now operate a drill with the best of them? Definitely. And in bare feet.

The question that has stuck with me all day—why did a little snafu with the screen door (I finally pitched the old one and installed the new one—almost) mean so much to me? I'm not sure. Maybe it was looking at the old one, weather beaten and broken. The screen flapping with remnants of packing tape used in an attempted repair. The latch was barely hanging on. It truly had seen better days. I don't remember it looking so worn out when I moved in here three years ago.

Then there was the new door, all shiny and fancy. It has a screen and a window. The handle lifts so the short people can get in and out easily. There's a closer instead of a hack job chain to stop the slamming and catching of humans in the door. It locks unlike most of the doors here. I bet it doesn't even make noise yet. And I put it up. Me.

That new door looks how I feel. New on the outside. Put together(ish) but still sporting the awkward stickers from the store. Finally out of the box and where it belongs. Keeping out what should stay out and letting in what belongs. But incomplete. It doesn't quite open or close. It will once I correct the problem, but it's going to take some work. For now, it's tied shut courtesy of an old Halloween costume and the inside knob of the front door. And what would make me smile the biggest would be to figure it out and make it right. To be able to open and close as it should, as I should. To filter what matters versus what doesn't. To start quitting the things that take up space with no return. And to really zero in on the things that stay.

That little blue eyed baby girl reached for me today. She didn't want anyone. She was whiny and frustrated…kind of like me. I sat her down in my lap, much like I wished someone would have done for me. She pulled her knees up and sank the back of her round little head into the softness of my neck. She snuggled in and let me hold her. I whispered some secrets in her ear and kissed her temple. She turned ever so slightly to look at me before hunkering back in. We sat like that until the demands of the other four required that we move.

These are the moments. These are the things that should fill the space of the days. They should be the things that we look back on to remember what love and life feel like. They are the settling of big feelings into something manageable that says you weren't created to install doors. You were created to love the hard ones. Because you can. And not because they're hard. But because they have moments of hard. And you get it.

Hours later as she drifted off to sleep in my arms, my eyes the last thing that she saw before hers closed for the night, I thanked God for the yesterdays and the todays. For the gift of innocence wrapped up in small people like her. For the bigger small people who told me 976 times that my door was so beautiful even though it didn't work and that I did a great job. For being brave enough to even consider installing a damn door by myself. For a year of transition that is leading into a year of self-discovery.

Come in through the garage.

The front door is a work in progress.

Ghost in the Appliances
by L.L. Barkat

I have never been one to like guns. My stepfather displayed his rifles on the living room wall (which frightened me), and I watched my mother pull a trigger once (the shotgun kickback threw her to the ground). We ate deer all winter, claimed by buckshot; I couldn't look when the deer lay silently in the back of the baby-blue pickup truck.

Despite my feelings about firearms, I am just now thinking of buying a pistol. Because, today, my stove unilaterally changed its clock to military time. I don't remember this option in the user's manual. (Just what, I ask, must a stove be planning, to take such measures?)

This week I have been dealing with clogged drains, a leaky ceiling, and even a flat tire on the way to the library. Thankfully, I have a Volvo, and, like the stove, it has a way with language. "Tire needs air now!" it silently observed, with a huge exclamation point above the message.

Sure enough, the Volvo was being forthright. The front tire *did* need air. I could see a nail with a little piece of my neighbor's roof still attached to it, slowly causing the car to communicate in exclamation points. I paid the service station down the street to remove the nail, with a gun-like implement, and patch up the tire. This calmed the Volvo considerably, and it has gone back to talking about the weather. ("It is 50 degrees today.")

I suppose I am overreacting just a little bit, but I can't help thinking that the stove has less honorable intentions than the car. I wonder if it is considering vengeance for the unjust treatment of its former kitchen companion—the old sink we left under the hemlocks. After all, we thought that location would simply be a temporary shelter. We thought we'd surely sell the Depression-era appliance at a good price, to a peaceful home.

The sink is (or was) white. It is made of iron and has a built-in washer board. The drain is filled with pine needles that are morphing into mud. Where the faucets used to be, there are two holes. Sometimes I imagine a woman's hands turning the long-gone faucets. I imagine her washing a piece of meat from an animal somebody may have shot. She turns and smiles. "Can't you see?" she seems to be asking.

I am not sure what she wants me to notice. Is it the ease with which she turns the straight handles? The way she doesn't have to worry that her sink will communicate with her, beyond a squeak in the left faucet? Does she want me to know that her husband shot the animal, and brought it home in a vehicle that only spoke in tail-pipe smoke signals?

She turns back to the sink, and I feel at a loss. I want to ask her, should I buy a pistol? Should I be afraid of the world I live in? Or should I just go to the basement, reset the kitchen fuse, and hope that the stove will surrender to Eastern Standard Time—without a fight.

1

What's It All About?

~

"An essay is valuable when it gives us a glimpse
into the authentic personality and core of a student,
a real aspect of the student's life that has played a role
in developing them into the person they are today.
That's important because we're admitting people,
not academic profiles or great stories."

– Nick Spaeth, Associate Vice President for Admission,
Monmouth College

"Don't write about your grades.
We are the experts at knowing how smart you are
and how you performed in high school.
The personal statement will help us understand
other areas of your life."

– Mike Cook, Senior Associate Director of Admissions,
Michigan State University

~

First Things First: Take It Off Your Stress List

As a private writing, reading, and college test prep tutor over the past 15 years, I've witnessed some…stress. Parents wanting their kids to study for the SAT as early as sixth grade. Students Skyping me between violin and swim practice to wrangle out topic sentences comparing Atticus Finch to Abraham Lincoln. Copies of *The Scarlet Letter* flung across the room in frustration. (Okay, I confess).

So why would I add to the academic anxiety by suggesting that high schoolers start thinking about their college applications as early as their junior, sophomore, or even freshman year?

Because the essence of a good college application essay isn't about learning the "secret," squeezing in a house-building trip to Haiti to have an impressive topic to write about, or working hard to get an edge on the competition. It's about being your best self. And it's never too early to be you.

Learn What It's About

You Beyond the Numbers

In the middle of all that data surrounding grades and test scores and class ranking, the essay is a chance to just be yourself. Isn't that a relief?

The Harvard Graduate School of Education recently released a report, "Turning the Tide," through the Making Caring Common project. This report details how and why colleges should work even harder on expanding the admissions process beyond statistics:

> . . .college admissions can send compelling messages
> that both ethical engagement—especially concern
> for others and the common good—and intellec-
> tual engagement are highly important.

In other words, sure, that 5 on your AP Spanish test is nothing to sneeze at. But neither is spending extended afternoons helping your grandmother in her garden. Or volunteering long-term (not just an afternoon or two for a quick "application filler") in a community literacy program. You were not created to perform, but to live. And living can't always be quantified.

Sarah Watkins, an admissions counselor at the University of Michigan, explains that "application essays are like student interviews, a chance to hear their voice" amidst a swirl of information.

Your essay is a chance to show the admissions counselors one glimmering slice of that life.

You as a Good Fit for the School

Students often see the essay as a persuasive tool to somehow talk a school into taking them. But have you ever thought that you might not want to be taken?

When you write an essay that is 100 percent you—quirks and all—and a college accepts you, you know you're headed to the right place.

But when you contort your personality and words into an essay tailor-made for a school, stripping any semblance of your true self, you might find yourself a stranger in a strange land when September hits.

Imagine you spend days getting ready for a party. You know one of the "cool kids" is going to be there, so you shop for clothes you don't normally wear, create playlists of bands you don't normally listen to, and get all the dirt on the people he doesn't like. You fake your way through the party and get his attention. Great! Now he wants to hang out.

The problem is, he's not really hanging out with you. Before long, you'll grow exhausted trying to fit into his world and return to the world you know and love—the world that loves you for who you are.

If you've done all you can to let your best self shine on the page, but you don't make it into that "dream" school, maybe that school wasn't so dreamy in the first place. For you. It could be perfect for your older sister or lab partner, but these four years are not about them. They are about (getting the theme here?) you.

You as a Writer

Finally, and importantly, schools want to see that you can write. Surprise: even if you're dead set on becoming a computer engineer and don't plan on reading a word of Austen for the rest of your life, you'll have to write in college. A lot.

The application essay gives colleges a chance to see not only how well you put your sentences together but how cohesively you can organize information and stick to a theme. Not all schools take the SAT and/or request the optional ACT essay, so this personal statement may be your only chance.

Besides, standardized test essays are written under a time crunch. The application essay can be polished to a shine.

"But wait!" Thou protesteth. "You just said this is about being 100 percent me! Shouldn't I just 'be myself,' write out my thoughts, and submit?"

As you'll discover in later chapters here, being yourself includes working hard on your writing. You can and should showcase your individual style, but you should also take the time and care to make it your very best.

Stress? No. Work? Yes. But with planning, strategy, and plenty of time, you'll find this among the best work you've done.

2

So What Kind of Writing is This?

~

"We should be able to pick your essay up off the floor and know it's yours."

– Mary Henry, Communications Manager for Enrollment Management, Purdue University

~

I know what you're thinking. Essays. Introductions opening with rhetorical questions and ending in thesis statements. Three body paragraphs, each supporting a main idea. A conclusion that sums it all up with a bow on top.

Don't you dare.

First of all, an essay like that, even with the fancy bow, is hardly a "gift" most human beings want to unwrap. Second of all, this is not the kind of essay admissions counselors find helpful. Sure, formulaic five-paragraph essays have their place— when you're first learning how to structure an argument as a beginning writer, for instance—but they aren't the only kinds of essays people write.

If you've had a chance to read the short essays featured in Chapter 1 or any of the books listed in Appendix A, you will have discovered the engaging, surprising world of short personal narratives. With rare exception, colleges are looking for this kind of storytelling arc in your main personal essay, not a cookie-cutter formula. Some of the best essays, according to Todd Iler, Senior Assistant Director of Admissions at Purdue University, "are written like a movie."

But, of course, it's not enough just to tell a story. If you strive to merely entertain your readers, they won't get a sense of your ability to analyze and reflect upon your experiences, the part of your application essay that demonstrates your personality, maturity, and fit for the school.

So I do not believe in a college essay formula, of course. But I do believe in some pretty important guidelines.

Let's start with what you should never, ever do.

Never, Ever Do These!

1) *Don't give them the "five-paragraph special"*

Just in case you didn't think I was serious. . . Nope. Don't do it. Get that five-paragraph mold out of your mind. Is it gone? Like really, really gone? Good.

2) *Don't rehash all the information from your application form*

That's what the application form is for. You don't have to squeeze in every last detail of your activities and coursework in the essay. In fact, if you do, admissions counselors will think you're just made of what you do instead of who you are. This is important. Schools want human beings, not accomplishment machines, joining their communities.

3) *Don't list all the reasons you're awesome*

Show, don't tell. You've heard it your whole life. And it applies to this essay process more than anything else. Instead of listing all your qualities (and I know you have a lot), choose one or two to illustrate with narrative. Stories, not abstractions, will stick in your reader's brain grooves.

4) *Don't be a kiss up*

Yes, you want to make connections between your life and your prospective school. But don't just flatter them. Beautiful campus, cutting-edge facilities, award-winning professors? Skip it. If your essay sounds like a brochure for the school, you've got an audience problem. They're already convinced.

Keith Gehres, Director of Outreach and Recruitment at The Ohio State University, agrees: "You can tell by the tone and language when students are writing trying to guess what we want to hear." But in those misdirected attempts, the genuine voice is lost. "I've read some essays," Gehres continues, "that I personally disagree with but have the authentic student's voice come through. We want those voices here. We need those voices here. We are a diverse student body."

5) *Don't beg for mercy*

You might have a moving, even sad, story to tell. That's okay, as long as the end goal of telling that story is showing the admissions department character, personality, and maturity. Telling a sob story, or, worse, coming out and pleading for admission, is off-putting to any college.

Now that we've gotten the no-no's out of the way, let's talk about the yes-yes's.

Yes, Yes, Always Do These!

1) *Make it Personal*

Does your essay tell a personal story? Does it have a voice? *Your* voice? Or can it be interchanged with an essay by Typical American College Senior? If you took your name off the essay and left it on your friend's or teacher's desk, would he or she be able to identify the writer?

2) *Make it Specific*

Later, we'll talk more about choosing topics. But my biggest one-word tip? Narrow. If you don't think your topic is narrow enough, it probably isn't. Also, if your story doesn't have a specific beginning and ending point (preferably in a time span that takes less than an hour) you may be left with a whole lot of vagueness—and boring, general language—on your hands.

Once, a student of mine wanted to write about his trip to Europe. Travel essays are risky in themselves (we will talk about that in Topics), but he insisted.

"Okay," I said. "We can give it a try. But narrow it down."

So he chose France.

"Smaller," I said.

"Paris?"

"Nope."

"The Louvre?"

"You're getting closer."

"The Mona Lisa?"

I gave him a sideways glance. "Everyone talks about the Mona Lisa when they talk about the Louvre."

"But that's the thing! I wasn't into the painting," he explained. "I liked another one in an adjoining gallery, a painting everyone else ignored for Mona."

And, boom: we had a topic.

3) *Make it Vivid*

You want your reader to enter into your story, not peer at it from the outside. While you don't want to include details just for details' sake, you need to engage the reader enough to want to emotionally invest in your story. This essay is ultimately about you, of course, not the swampy pulp of orange juice that stuck in your teeth that jittery first morning at your new school. But that swampy pulp is detailed enough to help me feel, and experience, your story with you. And make me want to read on.

4) *Make it Narrative*

Not an essay-essay. A story-essay. You know. In case you haven't gotten that idea yet.

5) *Make it Natural*

You're going to put a lot of time into this. A lot of drafts. You should. If there's ever a time to polish a piece of writing, it's now. However, this is not the time to try out your newest "impressive" vocabulary words or imitate James Joyce. As Mary Henry of Purdue says, "I like the real stuff. Students shouldn't try to sound like professors. Essays should be conversational and paint a picture."

It's a balance: sharp but informal; entertaining but analytical. Be you, but be the best *you*, you can be.

Getting an idea? In the next chapter, we'll look at a sample student essay and see how the writer brilliantly incorporates the yes-yes's above!

3

A Closer Look at a Winning Application

~

"I love essays that demonstrate all of the elements of good writing—clarity, organization, correct spelling and punctuation, and engaging prose—not to mention the flare of vivid descriptors, unexpected verbs and inspired narrative flow. When I encounter an essay that is clearly the product of someone who cares about their writing, it is a treat."

– Greg Orwig, Vice President of Admissions and Financial Aid, Whitworth University

~

In the last chapter, we looked at what the college essay is all about (and not about). Now, we're going to take a look at how a young man we'll call Ben—who has since graduated from his dream college and is starting his career—made the most of the College Essay Yes-Yes's in his own winning application.

Blue Jeans

An orange-striped polo shirt and a new pair of faded jeans stared me in the face as I looked in the mirror. I never knew a simple pair of clothes could cause such fear. I felt my heart pounding in my head as I thought about all the anxious moments I was about to encounter. As I buttoned the top of my shirt and zipped up my jeans, my hands shook and my fingers trembled. I felt the stitching of the shirt on my back and the fraying of the jeans on my legs. Everything had to be just right. Today would be my first day wearing a pair of jeans to school. I was in eighth grade.

Wearing jeans to school seems like the most natural thing a teenager can do. Most boys can wake up, put on a pair of jeans and a T-shirt, and walk out the door. Not me. My whole life I wore the same style Adidas sweatpants to school, always carefully tucking in a soft T-shirt with the tags removed. The familiar snug feeling of sweatpants tied tightly around my waist made me feel safe and secure. My friends often asked why I insisted on this strange habit. I always answered the same way: I wore clothes that felt most comfortable on my body.

I was born with Sensory Integration Disorder (SID), a neurological dysfunction that distorted how my nervous system processed and organized sensory information. I had particular trouble with noise, sensitivity to touch, and body awareness. Loud places like basketball games and playgrounds bothered me. Simple tasks like putting on a pair socks unnerved me. Wearing socks with seams felt like walking with sandpaper between my toes. I would rather walk around in shoes with no socks. Blue jeans? I hated the thought of wearing them. Without drawstrings to pull tightly, my body always thought they would fall off. Even if I wore a belt, I could not tolerate the insecurity. Wearing jeans not only represented physical discomfort, but change as well. I liked my routine of dressing in familiar sweats.

Yet, with each passing day of middle school, I thought more and more about the future. Could I really see myself as a 30-year-old man wearing a pair of baggy sweatpants? No. My girlfriend at the time giving me a little "hint" to wear jeans didn't help my cause. Besides, who wants to live their entire life looking like Steve Urkel? The guy made me laugh, but I didn't exactly consider him my role model. I knew the day would come when I would wear a pair of jeans to school, but it scared me to even think about it. Still, it was time to let go of what was comfortable, what felt right. Those few moments of terror when every student and staff member would stare at me (or so I thought) would seem like a speck of dust five years down the road. Then, I walked out my front door wearing a new pair of faded jeans.

That first time wearing blue jeans frightened me because it forced me out of my routine. I hated change and wearing jeans signified change in every sense of the word. I had never been more intimidated in my life. Yet, that day went by just like any other. No one laughed. No one stared. In fact, I received many compliments. I started that day anxious and afraid, but I walked out of school confident and proud.

As strange as it seems, wearing a pair of jeans to school helped me mature more than any other experience. I learned the benefits of change and the great opportunities that come each time I take on a challenge. Today, I can overcome pangs of anxiety in situations where I fear being laughed at or embarrassed. I embrace experiences such as addressing the Student Senate every Friday morning. Even being asked to sing Madonna's "Material Girl" for a recent interview in front of classmates and teachers could not faze me. I now realize that when I live fearlessly, I live most fully.

That first day wearing jeans, I gained much more than I lost. Hesitation, doubt, and the fear of change slowly disappeared, replaced by calmness and confidence. I found something within me I never knew I had: inner-strength and self-assurance. By committing to trying new things, I learned to overcome both the physical discomfort and emotional stress of putting myself out on a ledge, not knowing where it leads. Wearing blue jeans jump-started a change in my life. It led to many other experiences that made me a stronger, better person. Taking a risk and being fearless in stressful situations is no longer a burden. Now, I welcome these challenges with pride, energy, and security. I have the self-belief to reveal my character. All thanks to a faded pair of denim.

How Can You Write a Successful Essay Like Ben Did?

1) *Make It Personal*

Remember when I said you should be able to leave your essay on a teacher's or friend's desk without your name—but write it in such a way that he or she can identify your voice?

Ben doesn't hold back. He takes a risk by talking about a deeply-personal topic, sensory integration disorder, and owns that story with candor and confidence.

An interesting tidbit about Ben: during high school, he was a highly-ranked tennis player in his state. He had good grades and high test scores. He could have written an essay to "impress"—the A on the U.S. History final project or the "big match" that qualified him for state finals. But he logged those accomplishments on the application form and chose the route of vulnerability for his essay. He made his writing the place to be painfully, and delightfully, human.

2) *Make It Specific*

Ben doesn't chronicle his entire experience with sensory integration disorder. Instead, he narrows his topic down to one key event related to his challenges. However, the event Ben chooses is strategic, not arbitrary, as it signifies a turning point in his maturity and confidence. And guess what readers will remember after going through those thousands of essays? Yep. The faded pair of denim.

3) *Make It Vivid*

Numbers two and three are related. If you don't narrow your topic (more on this in the next chapter), you'll have trouble incorporating details as you attempt to cover too much ground in 500 words. Because Ben chose the "jeans day" as the main focus, he could include a number of sensory gems:

"I felt the stitching of the shirt on my back and the fraying of the jeans on my legs."

"The familiar snug feeling of sweatpants tied tightly

around my waist made me feel safe and secure."

"Wearing socks with seams felt like walking with sandpaper between my toes."

"Those few moments of terror when every student and staff member would stare at me (or so I thought) would seem like a speck of dust five years down the road."

"Even being asked to sing Madonna's 'Material Girl' for a recent interview in front of classmates and teachers could not faze me."

4) *Make It Narrative*

He can tell a story, right? As I emphasized in the last chapter, the college application essay shouldn't be a "three ways in which wearing blue jeans changed my life" format with a traditional thesis statement and topic sentences leading into body paragraphs arranged by main ideas.

This story has a beginning (anxiety about wearing jeans to school), middle (showing up in jeans) and end (learning and growing as a result of wearing them). The narrative structure serves to draw readers in because, well, everyone loves a good story.

5) *Make It Natural*

True, Ben is a good writer. He also wrote many, many drafts. But in the process of perfecting his essay, he never lost his sense of self: a seventeen-year-old boy. He refers to a television character from his childhood, Student Senate, and a middle-school girlfriend. He doesn't load up the essay with flashy vocabulary or scholarly references. He comes across as a teenager presenting himself in the best way possible—*himself* being the key word.

Are there any literary flaws in the essay? Sure. It was written by a high school student. But, submitting a masterpiece worthy of *The New Yorker* could be unwelcome, if not suspect.

Be yourself. And do your best job doing it.

4

Choosing a Topic

~

"Some of the most memorable topics have ranged from
a guy shaving his legs to play water polo, to cyber bullying,
to a student's attachment to his security blanket."

– Erin Moriarty, Director of Admissions, Loyola University

~

Depending on how many schools you're applying to, you'll
find a wide variety of essay prompts, some more open-ended
than others. While I won't be able to cover all the possibilities
here, I can give you an idea of the types of questions you may
encounter.

Common Application Questions

The Common App represents a network of more than 700
colleges that use the same online application so you don't have
to file separate paperwork for each school. In addition to the
usual questions about academic and extracurricular background, the Common App provides a prompt for one major
essay, around 500 words, that every school will receive.

These prompts were included in the 2016-2017 application:

1. Some students have a background, identity, interest, or talent that is so meaningful they believe their application would be incomplete without it. If this sounds like you, then please share your story.

2. The lessons we take from failure can be fundamental to later success. Recount an incident or time when you experienced failure. How did it affect you, and what did you learn from the experience?

3. Reflect on a time when you challenged a belief or idea. What prompted you to act? Would you make the same decision again?

4. Describe a problem you've solved or a problem you'd like to solve. It can be an intellectual challenge, a research query, an ethical dilemma—anything that is of personal importance, no matter the scale. Explain its significance to you and what steps you took or could be taken to identify a solution.

5. Discuss an accomplishment or event, formal or informal, that marked your transition from childhood to adulthood within your culture, community, or family.

The Coalition for Access, Affordability & Success Essay Prompts

Like The Common Application, the Coalition for Access,

Affordability & Success represents a network of colleges and universities that draw on the same main application. The following questions are listed for the 2016-2018 school years:

1. Tell a story from your life, describing an experience that either demonstrates your character or helped to shape it.

2. Describe a time when you made a meaningful contribution to others in which the greater good was your focus. Discuss the challenges and rewards of making your contribution.

3. Has there been a time when you've had a long-cherished or accepted belief challenged? How did you respond? How did the challenge affect your beliefs?

4. What is the hardest part of being a teenager now? What's the best part? What advice would you give a younger sibling or friend (assuming they would listen to you)?

5. Submit an essay on a topic of your choice.

Open-Ended Questions

Some schools keep their prompt pretty general, saying nothing more than "Please complete a one-page personal statement and submit it with your application." No matter how simple the prompt, however, you will want to respond with a specific, vivid, and personal essay. And if you're writing an essay for another school, including the Common App or Coalition? Good news: you can "double up" and use that essay to fulfill an open-ended prompt.

School-Based Questions

Many schools ask for a personal statement/Common Application or Coalition essay and an essay (or two or three) that requires you to describe your career goals and/or specific interest in the college or academic department of your major.

We will be looking at these school-specific questions more in depth in Chapter 7, but for now, a little bit of advice: research! Spend as much time as you can getting to know your prospective schools and majors before you apply. Your writing—and satisfaction of knowing you're applying to the right places—will show for it. Here are two examples of school-based questions:

1. Describe the unique qualities that attract you to the specific undergraduate College or School (including preferred admission and dual degree programs) to which you are applying at the University of Michigan. How would that curriculum support your interests?

2. Describe two or three of your current intellectual interests and why they are exciting to you. Why will Cornell's College of Arts and Sciences be the right environment in which to pursue your interests?

Oddball Questions

These questions are so clearly associated with specific schools, it may be hard to "double up" and modify your responses for others. Some schools, like University of Chicago, change their questions every year. And yes, they are always, well, weird. For example:

1. Consider something in your life you think goes unnoticed and write about why it's important to you. (University of Wisconsin-Madison)

2. What is square one, and can you actually go back to it? — Inspired by Maya Shaked, Class of 2018 (University of Chicago)

So How Do I Start?

Get Organized

Before you start brainstorming topics, get organized. Copy and paste all your essay prompts into a document, and color-code questions that are similar enough to allow for doubling up or modifying. Then determine how many total essay "concepts" you will have to come up with for the application process.

Don't skip this step! Doing this work at the beginning will save you from writing too many essays later. I mean, sure. I guess you can't have "too many" essays. But senior year presents enough challenges as it is. Save all that extra writing energy for college.

Choose a Topic

The brainstorming sheet on page 72 can help you choose a topic for the Common Application and many more open-ended questions. Even if the colleges of your choice offer prompts that take different directions, the brainstorming exercise will help you *reflect* on your qualities and experiences, a skill that's key to the success of your application process. And, you know, your life.

Brainstorming is just that—a quick list of ideas. But as you jot possible topics down, keep the following advice in mind:

Replace big, overused topics with smaller, more personal ones.

Students often believe they have to spin earth-shattering, dramatic yarns that leave their readers gasping for air. But you know what? Those "big" stories start to get pretty boring after student number 16,324 writes about the ginormous winning football game and hits "submit."

Keith Gehres of OSU describes one of the most memorable essays as a narrative about a student and his friend starting a My Little Pony fan club: "It's been years, and I still remember it. He talked about his development and growth as a cofounder of the club but told it with humor. He wasn't afraid to have some fun." Sarah Watkins of Michigan looks back fondly on an essay about how a student used cooking to relieve stress. The essay even included a recipe.

These topics aren't always the first to come to mind, though. How do you mine your experiences to find those topics that are both "small" and important?

Thinking you should write about The Big Service Trip to Mexico to show what you learned about Helping the Less

Fortunate? Why not write about your encounter with the woman who stocks the shelves at Walgreens? You know, when she snapped at you for talking too loudly on your phone and your argument turned into an opportunity for mutual understanding? There is power in the everyday, and admissions counselors want to see how you live those days. Because college will be composed of many "everydays."

Want to write about The Big Competition–whether won or lost–to show what you learned about Giving It Your Best? How about the story of your dad asking you to assemble the patio chairs before the barbeque? Remember how you had trouble making sense of the instructions but used your visual strength to adapt and solve the problem before the aunts and uncles showed up? Now that's interesting. They can look up your wrestling record later if they have to.

Think they want to hear your thoughts on a Big Issue like terrorism or the environment? These are undoubtedly important, but, let's face it: you're not thinking about it all that much. How about your thoughts about one of your quirky qualities? One of my favorite essays was how a student learned to live with–and eventually love–her wildly curly hair.

When in doubt, always go "small": quirky, local and personal—not big, dramatic, and vague. Your ability to reflect on what might otherwise appear to be a mundane event reveals growth, critical thinking, and maturity.

There are exceptions, of course. A student with a gap in his or her transcript may have some explaining to do. Admissions counselors want to give students the benefit of the doubt, but they need information to back that benefit up. Often, personal illness, deaths in the family, or divorce can have a significant negative impact on a student's performance. In those cases, an honest explanation of extenuating circumstances can help paint a complete picture of the student's human experience.

Todd Iler of Purdue tells about a student whose transcript showed a semester where she did very poorly in sharp contrast to other semesters. The student wrote an essay about her father's poor health: "He was losing his eyesight, and there was no mother in the picture. The student took it upon herself to drive her father to appointments to save his eyesight. That's a very real challenge. You don't want to hold that kind of thing against the student. We look for the bounce back."

Even with this serious event, however, the student didn't rely on the *event* to make the essay but her *ability to write about it* genuinely, with reflection. It always comes down to the student's voice.

Now, let's brainstorm! Come up with a list and get ready for our next chapter: how to begin writing about your topic.

5

Starting to Write

~

"Plan ahead. It's amazing how many essays are submitted
in the middle of the night."

– Keith Gehres, Director of Outreach and Recruitment,
The Ohio State University

~

You've organized your college application essay questions,
started brainstorming, and come up with a list of possibilities.
As you review your list, remember this advice about choosing
topics from the previous chapter:

When in doubt, always go "small": quirky, local, and personal—not big, dramatic, and vague. Got a list of at least three
good topics? Now it's time to write!

One of the biggest mistakes you can make at this point is
trying too hard *not* to make a mistake. That's where freewriting comes in, a practice I recommend for all types of writing,
from stories to essays to poems.

In fact, in my book *How to Write a Poem*, I define freewriting and discuss how it jumpstarts the beginning of the writing process. Most of this discussion applies to drafting the
college application essay, too:

Peter Elbow, author of *Writing Without Teachers*, coined the term "freewriting" in 1975. You may have tried it before: setting aside a certain amount of time, say, five to fifteen minutes, during which you write your thoughts without stopping, censoring, or editing in any way. The thinking behind taking this all-important first step? Preserving your voice, the lifeblood of your writing:

The habit of compulsive, premature editing doesn't just make writing hard. It also makes writing dead. Your voice is damped out by all the interruptions, changes, and hesitations between the consciousness and the page. In your natural way of producing words there is a sound, a texture, a rhythm—a voice—which is the main source of power in your writing. I don't know how it works, but this voice is the force that will make a reader listen to you. Maybe you don't like your voice; maybe people have made fun of it. But it's the only voice you've got. It's your only source of power.

So let's get going with your essay.

Freewrite

This is your first opportunity to get your thoughts down. It's exciting to think that your finished product will one day have these first few minutes to thank! But no pressure, really. This part of the process is truly "free." Here's what you'll do:

1) Choose one item from your list of brainstormed topics.

Remember, it should be a specific, personal incident.

2) Set a timer for 7 minutes.

3) Write on your topic until the timer goes off. The only rule? Write nonstop and don't censor yourself. But DO focus on details and senses.

4) When the timer goes off, shake out your hand and take a break, at least 15 minutes, before continuing to the next step.

Highlight

Most likely, you won't want to use everything from your freewrite. This is your chance to isolate those most important parts that came from your gut, the hidden soul of your topic that will give your essay the "youness" to make it shine. Here's what you'll do:

1) Read through your freewrite.

2) Highlight passages and sentences–even just words or phrases–that are vivid, essential, surprising, or "home-hitting" in some way.

3) If absolutely nothing hits you, repeat the freewriting process with one of your other topics then try the highlighting exercise again.

Outline

Using your highlights, build an outline. Don't worry about Roman numerals and letters. This is just a simple plan to get you started with a basic structure. Here's what you'll do:

1) Rewrite or type the highlighted sections from your freewrite. Remember "Blue Jeans"? Some highlighted portions from the original freewrite may have looked like this:

felt the stitching of the shirt on my back and the fraying of the jeans on my legs

Today would be my first day wearing a pair of jeans to school. I was in eighth grade and had SID.

Without drawstrings my body always thought they would fall off.

I hated change and wearing jeans was a change.

looked like Steve Urkel

I had never been more intimidated in my life but no one laughed or stared. I received many compliments.

I started that day anxious and afraid, but I walked out of school confident and proud.

I found something within me I never knew I had: inner-strength and self-assurance.

2) List the main events of the story you're going to tell, then weave in the highlighted "hot spots," even if they're specific details. You don't want to forget them; those significant freewrite favorites really get at the heart of things!

The main events in "Blue Jeans" would look like this:

–anxious about wearing jeans to school
–background of clothes and SID
–would I always dress this way?
–time to take a risk
–the day went well

And here they are with the highlights woven in:

–anxious about wearing jeans to school

felt the stitching of the shirt on my back and the fraying of the jeans on my legs

Today would be my first day wearing a pair of jeans to school. I was in eighth grade and had SID.

–background of clothes/sensory integration disorder

Without drawstrings my body always thought they would fall off.

<u>I hated change and wearing jeans was a change.</u>

—would I always dress this way?

<u>looked like Steve Urkel</u>

—time to take a risk
—the day went well

<u>I had never been more intimidated in my life but no one laughed or stared. I received many compliments.</u>

3) Next, list the main points you'd like to include in the reflective portion of your essay. Remember, a good story without personal reflection is just a good story that doesn't show your ability to analyze. The main reflective points in "Blue Jeans" would look like this:

    —learned to embrace change
    —don't worry about being embarrassed (announcements, singing)
    —found inner strength

And here they are with the highlights woven in:

    —learned to embrace change

    —don't worry about being embarrassed (announcements, singing)

I started that day anxious and afraid, but I walked out of school confident and proud.

–found inner strength

I found something within me I never knew I had: inner-strength and self-assurance.

Write a First Draft

Now that you have an outline, it's time to turn it into a draft. The outline, of course, will inform the structure of your writing. But remember these two key tips:

- Generally speaking, a good pattern to follow as a guideline is Narrate your story, Reflect on your story, Connect what you learned from the story to other life events, and Full-Circle the ending back to the beginning narration ("all thanks to a faded pair of denim").

- Always think, *Small events, Big thoughts.*

Get ready, get set, and write your best you!

6

Revising, Editing, and Proofreading

~

"Small mistakes show you haven't done
your homework. Make sure you have your acronyms
and vernacular correct. And watch out for mixing up
the names of schools in your essay!"

– Sarah Watkins, Admissions Counselor,
University of Michigan

~

Congratulations! You've written the first draft of your college application essay. While you still have work ahead of you, the most mentally taxing part—coming up with your initial story and reflection—is done. Now it's time to polish your story to a shine.

Writers often confuse *revising*, *editing*, and *proofreading*. Let's quickly review the difference among these three important tasks, for they will all need your attention:

1. Revise: To improve the content of your writing, from adding (or removing) details, to reorganizing ideas, to sometimes changing your focus completely. The process of revision is, literally, "re-envisioning" your work to ensure it plumbs the heart of your message.

2. Edit: To improve the writing itself, as in sentence structure, word choice, and clarity. Editing focuses more on mechanics than big-picture content, though a well-edited piece will lend interest, voice, and credibility to your work.

3. Proofread: To check for typos, spelling, punctuation, and those other "little" mistakes that aren't so little, like forgetting to replace "Emory" with "Tufts" when you modify an essay. Careful proofreading shows you care about your work and respect your readers.

I'm often asked to "proofread" a first draft of an essay when it is actually several drafts away from that step. At minimum, you should take your paper through at least two major passes first: revising and editing.

Revising Your First Draft

During the revision process, read through your essay and address the following crucial questions about content:

1. Does your essay answer the question? Remember, even the most splendid piece of writing won't impress admissions officers if you've failed to give them what they asked for.

2. Does your essay balance story with reflection? Or, in the

case of a school-specific essay, does it balance your personal experience with research about your prospective major or department? Too many facts without narrative structure or personal connections makes for a boring essay. Too much story without any reflection or research makes for an irrelevant one.

3. Does your essay show, not tell? You've heard it from teachers since elementary school. But we wouldn't keep saying it if writers, from kindergartners to professional novelists, didn't need reminding from time to time.

Often when I advise a student to add detail to his or her essay, I hear, "I'm already at the 500-word limit!"

But adding more detail doesn't necessarily mean adding more words to the piece. Think about replacing vague sentences with specific ones, general descriptions with concrete examples.

For instance, our "Blue Jeans" author originally wrote a sentence like, "Socks were very uncomfortable to wear." Instead of adding more sentences, he replaced it: "Wearing socks with seams felt like walking with sandpaper between my toes." The image and simile communicate discomfort much more vividly by calling upon our senses.

4. Does your essay need trimming? Sometimes you'll need to cut your essay to meet the word count. Sometimes you'll need to cut it simply to make it a better piece of writing. These factors work together. Admissions officers put word limits on application essays not only to manage their own time but to ensure focused, high-quality writing. "Usually an essay is too long," says Ineliz Soto-Fuller, Director of Undergraduate Admis-

sions at Seattle Pacific University. "The more students edit, the more they see parts that can be more concise and punchy and get to the point."

There's no formula for cutting, but many writers fall into similar habits when writing early drafts. Watch out for these:

• **Taking a while to get started.** Often you can cut the first paragraph, if not the first several, because they were just "warm up" to begin with.

• **Using too many adjectives** to describe a noun when one modifier, or none, would suffice. Watch out for those adjective clusters! Do you need "I watched the cool, blue, sparkling water" when "The waves shimmered" works just as well—or better?

• **"Doubling up" on sentences.** Writers commonly state ideas twice in early drafts, almost as if the rhythm helps them process their thoughts. This kind of processing is important, but it doesn't have to go to print.

Consider this passage: "I realized taking the time to solve a conflict with my sister was just as important as studying for the test. Talking to her about the problem took priority over my grade." Do you really need both sentences? Can you cut one of them or combine wording and ideas from both?

Editing Your Revised Draft

It may take two or three revisions to get your draft to where you need it. Once you feel happy about the content, you can move along to editing, or sentence-level polishing:

1) Cleanse of clichés. *Clichés*. Even the best writers look into the limpid pools of their eyes and fall captive to their charms. (See?) Beware of those college essay favorites, like "the school of my dreams," "opportunity of a lifetime," "I went all out," "determined to succeed," "on the right path," and "whatever I put my mind to." Chances are, if you've heard the phrase before, it's a cliché.

2) Vary sentence length and structure. Watch out for a series of sentences that uses the same word count, structure, or subject and verb, unless you're purposely employing parallel structure.

Sometimes it helps to chart a paragraph. Make a table in which you list the number of words and the main subject and verb (or the first subject and verb) in each sentence. Do you find several sentences that start with "I"? Or use the boring verb "was"? Or fall into the same number of words?

Suppose Ben charted the second paragraph of his essay:

> Wearing jeans to school seems like the most natural thing a teenager can do. Most boys can wake up, put on a pair of jeans and a T-shirt, and walk out the door. Not me. My whole life I wore the same style Adidas sweatpants to school, always carefully tucking in a soft T-shirt with the tags removed. The familiar snug feeling of sweatpants tied tightly around my waist made me feel safe and secure. My friends often asked why I insisted on this strange habit. I always answered the same way: I wore clothes that felt most comfortable on my body.

Sentence	No. of Words	Subject	Verb
1	14	wearing	seems
2	19	boys	wake
3	2	–	–
4	23	I	wore
5	17	feeling	made
6	11	friends	asked
7	16	I	answered

Repetition can make your writing sound stilted. Ben, however, varies his sentence lengths by leaping from 19 to 2 and back up to 23. He also varies his subjects and verbs to avoid losing his reader in a sea of "I's" and "am's."

Take your writer on an adventure of linguistic swoops and turns, not a lethargic walk. Vary word choice. Keep your eye out (you can even use your word processor's search function) for words that keep popping up, like *goals*, *success*, *future*, and, well, *college*. Read your work aloud, too. You may be surprised by what you hear.

Proofreading Your Edited Draft

The last, but very important, step is to tidy up your essay for the fancy party at the admissions office.

We won't be covering grammar and punctuation rules here, but I strongly recommend consulting the Purdue Online Writing Lab for a clear and comprehensive review.

Should your essay be perfect? As close as you can get it. Ask a few trusted, detail-oriented readers to give it a read (just for proofreading at this point, as you've already done all the writing, revising, and editing). And read your essay aloud at least a couple more times.

Some items to especially keep in mind are the following:

- Capitalization
- Spelling/homonyms
- Fragments, unless used intentionally and strategically as a part of your voice
- Run-ons
- Plurals/possessives
- Commas, semicolons, colons

If you've revised, edited, and proofread to the best of your ability, you are ready to–shall we say it?–hit "submit"!

7

School-Specific Essays

~

"This essay is your chance to show you've done
the intellectual legwork for why you want to study your
major and how you've explored that interest."

– Charles Murphy, Associate Director of Admissions,
University of Illinois, Urbana-Champaign

~

Even though over 700 colleges take advantage of the convenient
Common Application (with the newer Coalition Application's
network growing every year), many of them want to know
more: namely, why are you applying to their schools? Have you
given their academic programs much thought, or are you just
checking a name off a list?

In these cases, individual schools will ask you to write
"supplement" essays that typically answer why you want to
apply to that school, what you plan on choosing for a major,
and how that school will help you work toward your professional
goals. Schools that don't use a universal application may also
ask you to write an essay that answers the question, "Why *us*?"

These essays are very different from the autobiographical
essays students write for their main personal statements.

Rather than tell a story, they connect students' specific needs to specific college offerings. That doesn't mean the essay needs to be boring, though. Even "straightforward" writing can benefit from personal anecdote and imagery.

Take a look at this essay from Eric, a student who responded to Northwestern University's version of the "why" prompt:

What are the unique qualities of Northwestern—and of the specific undergraduate school to which you are applying—that make you want to attend the University? In what ways do you hope to take advantage of the qualities you have identified? (300 words max)

Hordes of rotting carp drifted on the surface of the water. Smoke fumed out of the factory chimneys as chemical-filled water entered the stream. This is a horrifying, yet common sight for rural Chinese cities like Guiyu. Due to the lack of environmental regulation, pollution devastates the area. As I visited Guiyu, I found the ecosystem, the organisms that live there, and the children who splashed in the water to be an unbearable sight.

Leaving the scene, I felt compelled to change this situation. Transforming energy and matter to benefit the world has become my dream. After researching various schools, I have concluded that Northwestern's Chemical Engineering program will best help me in this pursuit. Northwestern's curriculum will not only educate me in the field of engineering, but provide design and communications courses to further my presentation and organizational skills, helping me connect with other chemical engineers to share ideas and collaborate effectively. Furthermore, the opportunity to select a theme within social science and humanities will allow me to take international relation courses to develop my ability to work within a range of cultures.

Aside from the required curriculum, Northwestern boasts many summer research opportunities that will connect me with professionals. For example, the Research Experience for Undergraduate programs provides students 10-12 weeks of real-life research with a professor or a company. Additionally, the Pura Playa project in the Engineers for a Sustainable World program allows students to create solutions to combat the plastic epidemic that plagues our oceans. By joining this program, I can collaborate with other engineers to create solutions to increase the efficiency of reusing resources.

The combination of courses, relationships and summer programs will become quintessential in developing my career. Northwestern will equip me with the means to eradicate the "Guiyus" of the future.

Eric provides plenty of specific detail about how and why Northwestern will help him meet his goal of becoming a chemical engineer: the curriculum, courses, and research opportunities. But he doesn't settle for *bland*. Eric frames the essay with an anecdote about his tragic visit to Guiyu, China, where he encountered the environmental degradation that inspired him to choose engineering as a major. By opening and closing with this imagery briefly, he not only makes the essay personal, but memorable, all while providing relevant analysis that shows the substance behind his decision to apply.

Preparing to Write

The "why" essay is all about research. Many students fall into the trap of describing why they *love* a school versus how, specifically, that school will *help* them. Remember, the people reading your essay most likely already agree their school is great. They don't need your praise. What they do need is your thorough understanding of how their institution will help you accomplish your goals.

Here are the steps you should take to prepare to write the "why" essay:

1) *Decide on a major*

Most school-specific prompts will ask about your academic goals. If you're leaning toward a field of study, write about it even if you're not one hundred percent sure. No one is going to check the essay you wrote as a high school senior when you graduate from college: *Wait. Four years ago he wrote about majoring in anthropology, and now he's getting a philosophy degree? Take back his diploma!* Having a specific major in mind will obviously make this process easier.

But what if you're leaning nowhere—are truly undecided? I've worked with students who have written successful essays in this case by treating their undeclared state as a major of its own, researching the support and services schools offer for undecided students.

2) *Go online. Really online.*

Of course you're going to go online to get your information. But rather than settle on the general information listed under "Prospective Student" pages, go to the department page of your major of interest. Read about the curriculum, courses, internships, and extracurricular opportunities. Read press releases, articles, and anything else you can access relating to the biology, English, or sports management people you hope to join soon. Taking a long time? Good. That means you're doing it right rather than skimming the surface for generalities.

3) *Create a template*

You will most likely be required to write several versions of the "why" essay, depending on where you're applying. Most students find it helpful to create a template of sorts they can modify for each school. Eric's sample essay follows this model:

- Opening anecdote that connects personal experience to professional goals

- Transition to what the school has to offer in terms of major/curriculum

- Examples of related opportunities outside the classroom (internships, summer programs, clubs)

- Ending that briefly summarizes and connects back to the opening anecdote

The details in paragraphs 3 and 4 will change for each school, but the opening and closing will most likely stay the same. Even transitional phrases can be retained from essay to essay. When applying to a long list of colleges, every little time saver makes a difference!

4) *Don't write them a brochure*

It's tempting, in all your enthusiasm, to praise a school for its beautiful campus, exciting location, and excellent academic reputation.

While these factors are important, your reader has heard them before, probably thousands of times. Great cities, sports teams, and magazine rankings attract students and improve the overall school experience. But when it comes to your success as a student, it boils down to the day-to-day: the classes you're sitting in, the people you're working with, and the jobs or graduate schools you're working toward. Most employers care more about what you *did* with your college time rather than where you went. It would be better to attend a school ranked 45th than 3rd if 45th U offers you the academic, leadership, and community opportunities closely aligned with your goals.*

---

* In his book *Outliers: The Story of Success*, Malcolm Gladwell notes that the last fifty Nobel Prize winners in Medicine and Chemistry graduated from schools like

In the process of researching for the "why" essay, many students discover that the school they thought they wanted to apply to—the one their parents and friends have been raving about—actually offers very little in their subject of interest while a "forgotten" school ends up becoming a hidden gem that makes all the difference.

Antioch College, Augsburg College, Berea College, City College of New York, Gettysburg College, Grinnell College, Hamilton College, Holy Cross, Hope College, Hunter College, Ohio Wesleyan University, Rice University, Rollins College (Florida), Union College (Kentucky), University of Dayton (Ohio), University of Florida, University of Illinois, University of Massachusetts, University of Minnesota, University of Nebraska, University of North Carolina, University of Notre Dame, University of Pennsylvania, University of Texas, Washington State University, and others. Only three of the fifty recipients graduated from MIT, two from Harvard, two from Columbia, and one from Yale—while two also graduated from City College of New York. Gladwell concludes that to be a Nobel Prize winner, you would have to get into a college "at least as good as Notre Dame or University of Illinois. That's all."

8

Final Thoughts

~

I've invited you to work hard on a process that, in many ways, will seem like one of the most important tasks of your life.

It is.

And, also, it isn't.

The college application journey does take time and will affect your future. But the promise of lifelong success doesn't rise or fall on one standardized test, grade, recommendation, or—yep—essay.

Remember that "C-" you earned in Spanish the year your mom got really sick? That "C-" is not who you are. It's one small piece of a complex life.

Remember that near-perfect score you got on your ACT? Congratulations! It might earn you a scholarship or two. But will it land you your dream job if you haven't enjoyed learning and connecting with other people throughout your life? Nope.

But what if you are good with people but scored poorly on the test? Are you doomed to an adulthood of dead-end dreams? Uh-uh.

There was your sophomore year, when you set the league record in the 100m hurdles. That will look great on your application. But as a junior you had to quit because you tore your knee. It's okay. Maybe you learned a few things about patience. Maybe you took up reading poetry and now think more deeply about the world.

What if you ditched class? Or worked two jobs? Or took care of your siblings? Or spent so much time playing guitar you ran out of time to volunteer?

Some parts of your high school life could've been better. Some, no doubt, could've been worse. The key now is to figure out who you've become and move forward as the best *you* you can be.

I've met some students who've gotten so nervous about writing their college application essay they can barely talk themselves down enough to type a word. Sure it's important, but it's also not *that* important. Here are a few final tips to help you keep perspective:

• The essay is just one piece of the process

• All you are responsible for, *in this moment*, is being yourself and doing your best

• If you can do that, you'll end up at a college right for you—not for your friends, parents, or Instagram followers, but *you*. Shouldn't your college community want you as much as you want them?

• The time you spend writing now is time well spent no matter what: learning about college, majors, storytelling skills, personal reflection, revision, editing, and sentence structure—most of all, yourself—is valuable on its own

• As I said back in Chapter 2, with planning, strategy, and plenty of time, you'll find this essay to be among the best work you've done

So relax, get perspective, and write your butt off. Then submit your application and relax again. You've got this.

Four years from now, will you let me know how everything went?

Appendix A

How to Write a College Application Essay: The Inspiration

~

The writers represented in the essay collections noted below explore, and make meaning from, specific memories and experiences, the bedrock of college application essays.

Brief Encounters: A Collection of Contemporary Nonfiction, edited by Judith Kitchen and Diane Lenney

Short Takes: Brief Encounters with Contemporary Nonfiction, edited by Judith Kitchen

In Brief: Short Takes on the Personal, edited by Mary Paumier Jones and Judith Kitchen

In Short: A Collection of Brief Creative Nonfiction, edited by Mary Paumier Jones and Judith Kitchen

Appendix B

Common App Open-Ended Essay Topic Brainstorming Worksheet

~

Respond to these questions with as much detail as possible. Complete sentences are not required, but be as precise as you can with your ideas.

Think of events that have clear beginnings and endings, not general time periods.

For instance, "The summer I entertained my cousins" is too broad. Think more along the lines of "The afternoon I created a relay race for my cousins to keep them from fighting."

1) List 3-5 important traits or characteristics that make you YOU.

2) Choose one of these traits. What memories from your life best illustrate how you developed or demonstrated this trait? Be specific!

3) List your "top" (most likely the most memorable) 3-5 failures. List specific incidents.

4) List 2-3 times when you challenged a belief or idea. Think about experiences in the home, classroom, and community.

5) List 2-3 problems you have solved. How did you solve them? Don't forget the "small" problems of everyday life. Solving those are often the hardest!

6) List 2-3 problems you would like to solve. How would you solve them? Again, don't overlook the everyday challenges!

7) Think of events or accomplishments that have served as bridges from childhood to adulthood. Think beyond formal events (graduations, etc.). What informal, even unexpected accomplishments, showed you were entering the next stage of life?

Appendix C

Sample Essays

~

Sample Personal Statements

The following real student essays were written in response to the Common Application, the Coalition Application, and other personal statement prompts. Names have been shortened and sometimes changed to protect the privacy of students sharing personal information. College graduation information (whether the student ended up attending the school he or she wrote the essay for) is provided to inspire you.

You will notice a wide range of topics and styles—as many as there are individual voices. These students did a fantastic job painting self-portraits with prose. Let them inspire you to be your best you!

Communication in Training

Eric C., University of Illinois, Urbana-Champaign 2019

The train screeched to a halt, and the doors hissed as hydraulic pumps cranked open the steel doors. Immediately, hordes of people charged in and out of the cart. People frantically tried to reach the doors—maids grasping groceries and men dressed in business suits. Bags smacked against my shins, and suitcases bruised my legs during a symphony of chaos. After this onslaught, I noticed a frail elderly woman clutching her cane as she slowly placed her shopping bags on the ground. I gestured to the old lady to take my seat. She smiled and thanked me.

This train—the MTR—is part of Hong Kong's public transportation system. It became an essential part of my life, intertwining with my schedule. Few people would regard a hectic rush hour as serene; however, every day I would enter those doors and cross into a state of tranquility.

After the woman sat down, she asked what I was doing out so late on the MTR by myself. I replied that my friend and I had been working on a school project. She praised me for my independence at the age of 11. "I was trapped by my parents, unable to travel freely. I envy your life," she said. She kept on recounting her life: "During World War II, my family and I clung to our lives. However, when Hong Kong was liberated I obtained a newfound sense of freedom. I was able to walk the streets without cowering in fear. I could buy any produce I wanted without restrictions; I could feed my family." I was mesmerized by her story; however, before I could reply, she stood up, patted my back, and said, "Whatever you do, cherish your freedom and keep on persevering."

This encounter showed me that I had been unaware of my freedoms, especially mobility. From socializing with my friends to commuting to school, I never once realized how much I relied on the train. This train created a sense of pleasantness for me. However, I also learned that this train provides a bond in the community. Talking with an elder despite our different upbringings and age disparity without feeling a sense of awkwardness defines the MTR system. In fact, all types of people from different social classes can talk to each other: construction workers and businessmen discussing the football match, store clerks and students raving about the new video game. Communicating without barriers creates a sense of comfort and contentment, since no one suffers from prejudice. The train has motivated me, now a citizen of the United States, to become an equalizer in my community.

For the past three years, I have been teaching English to Chinese elders who want to speak with their grandchildren and fully immerse themselves in society. In addition, I tutor struggling math students so they can compete with others who have an innate talent for math. As a prospective college student, I hope I can continue my work as an equalizer by aiding international students. Even though I don't ride the train anymore, I can still hear the businessman and construction worker laughing, connecting with each other at the end of the day.

A School to Call Home

Natalie S., Montana State University 2020

"So where do you go to school?"

For most people, it's an easy question. But for me, it was never that simple.

"I'm homeschooled," I would say after a moment of hesitation.

That answer never felt quite right. Saying "I'm homeschooled" sounded like my education was being done to me. And that couldn't be further from the truth. So this past summer, when asked "Where do you go to school?" I decided to change my answer.

"I'm a homeschooler."

Homeschooling is a choice I make every day. Saying I'm a homeschooler better conveys that I'm choosing my education for myself.

Choosing to be a homeschooler has allowed me to embrace all the aspects of who I am, one of which is a gardener. When I'm outside, covered in dirt, my back aching and spring wind whipping my hair into my face, I feel alive and certain that this is what I'm made to do. Because I'm a homeschooler, I choose to spend many hours in my gardens. I prepare the soil with dark, crumbly compost and watch as soil-enriching cover crops flood over the ground like luscious green waves. In early spring, I battle frigid Chicago weather with cloth and metal hoops, defending my seeds and my desire to finally eat fresh garden vegetables after the long winter. When I lift the low tunnel cloth, I see the baby green leaves bubbling up from the soil, cradled in mild warmth as the rest of the world continues to shiver within over-stuffed parkas. And a few weeks later, I rejoice in my triumph over the everlasting winter with a victory salad.

Because I'm a homeschooler, gardening is more than a hobby; it's also a big part of my curriculum. Every morning I can decide if it's a day for reading and research or for getting my hands dirty in the garden. Homeschooling not only allows me to choose how I spend my time, but also to choose to learn about topics that inspire and impassion me. When I was thirteen, I chose to take an online class called "Real Food, Nutrition and Health." I wanted to learn about healthy eating to supplement my learning through gardening. The course taught me about a good diet, but it also opened my eyes to something bigger.

Before that class, I had never heard the term "sustainable agriculture." I had never realized that there was a movement advocating for a change in the way we grow food. The idea that farming could not only minimize harmful impacts on the environment, but also heal the land, seized my attention. From there I couldn't stop, and my freedom of choice as a homeschooler propelled me to continue. I read articles and books, watched documentaries, and visited sustainable farms. I incorporated sustainable agriculture into my other studies as well. I wrote papers about sustainable livestock production, made connections between chemistry and soil composition, and supplemented discussions about genetically modified crops with studies about genetics.

Just as I have chosen to be a homeschooler, I choose the sustainable food and farming movement. I choose to make sustainable agriculture a part of my everyday learning, to pursue it in my studies in college, and to teach others about the power they have to choose what they eat. Someday I will have my own sustainable farm, and I imagine working on that farm, caring for livestock and harvesting vegetables, dirt covering my body and my back aching. And I will remember that making gardening and sustainable agriculture such a big part of my life was a choice, a choice made possible because I chose to be a homeschooler.

A Tightrope Walker's Final Trick

Meghan D., University of Illinois, Urbana-Champaign 2019

I attempted to wipe the sweat off my hands while I nervously looked down at the four-inch piece of wood. I knew that if I was going to do this, I would have to talk myself into it. It was only a back handspring, a skill I mastered while everyone else mastered riding their bikes. Every muscle in my body knew how to do it, so why couldn't my brain? I could feel the beam become slippery from the sweat that dripped off my body. I took a deep breath. I had to do this.

Jump a few years back to eighth grade, when I was making significant progress on my gym's competition team. I was known throughout the gym for being one of the best at the uneven bars—Illinois Uneven Bar State Champion three years in a row. But the balance beam was the bane of my existence. The troubles began when we had to begin going backwards on it. The beam seemed to transform from a wide four inches to a tightrope, one I could no longer easily walk. I had run into a huge mental block. Maybe it was because of the many times I had crotched the beam, or maybe it was because I couldn't hurl my body and hope for the best. Whatever the case, I had realized the dangers of going backwards on such a small, and not to mention high up, surface. And for a gymnast, realizing the danger of executing a skill is a recipe for disaster.

Two back handsprings in a row petrified me. I was determined to find a different skill that still met the requirements, so I decided to read up on the guidelines for my level. Instead of doing two back handsprings in a row, I chose to do a roundoff back handspring (which in hindsight I realize is a much scarier trick to do on a beam). In order to convince myself to do it, I became an architect. I stacked the mats around the beam in various positions, anything from a pyramid to a tower. I knew if I slowly decreased the height of the mats around the beam, then I wouldn't get nearly as frightened. But my mat-building skills were not enough.

Without a mat to psychologically coax me, I was never able to execute the skill. Maybe I would have mastered it if I hadn't shattered my knee, ending my gymnastics career. But what I didn't gain in skill level, I gained in personal abilities. At my old gym, every gymnast basically followed the same skill path to level ten, except me. I learned to adapt to my situation, a skill that influences my way of life. For example, if people become ill after donating blood at the Buffalo Grove Blood Drive where I volunteer, I can easily adapt to their specific situations and get them whatever they need. I'm can also construe a different way to approach a math problem if a teacher requires multiple ways to a solution. But most impressively, I can adapt to Chicago's unforgiving winters gracefully from Indian summers.

Despite the fact that I failed, I ultimately view my balance beam experience as a success. Although I did not succeed at what I had originally planned to accomplish, I learned to walk the thinner tightrope of adapting.

It Comes With the Territory

Ty G., University of Wisconsin-Madison 2021

A typical school night for me is not always smooth sailing. When 8 o'clock rolls around and my medication wears off, my night transitions from calm to chaos. Despite having eaten dinner less than two hours ago, I become ravenous like a participant in the Hunger Games. Aside from my insatiable hunger, my brain feels like the clothes inside of a washer: shifting and spinning in all directions. It becomes nearly impossible to focus on my nightly homework. Although this all may sound dramatic, it goes with the territory of having a neurological disorder called ADHD.

When I was younger, I felt embarrassed about taking medication to treat my ADHD. I never told my friends, and I didn't even want my parents to tell my teachers. Once, in third grade, I forgot to take my pill on the day of the AIMS standardized test. I panicked and called my dad to swiftly, but secretly, bring my medicine to school so I could focus. Without that pill, I knew it would be a struggle to even complete the test. I ended up scoring in the 99th percentile for Arizona students in both the math and reading sections. It was a turning point to realize that my medication for ADHD is nothing to be ashamed of but is rather a catalyst for bringing out the best version of me.

Although ADHD comes with various challenges, it also amplifies certain qualities such as visualization and creativity. Golf, a sport I chose at the age of eight, requires patience, focus, and consistency. While it may seem like having ADHD would be detrimental to my golf game, ironically, it has enhanced my mental capabilities. My ability to visualize has allowed me to develop an effective pre-shot routine during which I imagine the ball's flight ultimately reaching the target. Further, my creativity has helped me engineer shots that the average golfer may not undertake, such as a low hook-shot around a tree or a sky-high lob wedge over a tall saguaro cactus.

School is another venue in which my ADHD contributes to my unique thinking. For example, in math class, the majority of students may solve a problem in a traditional method, but sometimes I follow a different path to achieve the same correct answer. A recent case of this occurred in AP Statistics. A problem asked how to use stratified sampling to choose eight random apartments from an apartment building with nine floors containing four apartments on each floor. The entire class answered, "choose eight random floors and select one apartment per floor," but I devised a different answer. I wrote, "Stratify by columns of the apartment complex, selecting two random apartments per column, which would add up to a total of eight apartments." Although both answers received full credit, technically, my answer was more correct because in stratified sampling, all of the groups should be sampled from, not just eight out of the nine. This creativity and unique thinking allows me to contribute an unconventional perspective to the world around me.

Having had incredible success in school and golf, I no longer believe in the stigma of ADHD. I have learned to embrace my identity and have discovered that character is built by overcoming challenges and making the most of differences. The lasting remedy for my ADHD is not the medication but rather my attitude and determination to not only hurdle this obstacle but all others that stand in my way.

A Knack for Teaching

Kasia A., Purdue University 2020

"Try it again. It's an easy rhythm, Nikolai. Oh, and please sit down!" I said exasperatedly as I tried to rearrange my student's fingers on the piano. While Nikolai peered at the music, and fumbled over the notes, I realized two things. We were both frustrated, and I was about ready to give up. He had been struggling for months on the same song, with the same mistakes, and he wouldn't sit down on the piano bench.

As Nikolai began "Knick Knack Paddywack" for what seemed like the hundredth time, I could hear the clicking of his teeth in a futile attempt to keep the tempo, while his mother's frustration rose with each wrong note. It wasn't that Nikolai was unwilling to learn, on the contrary he listened very well. Rather, whatever I taught him stayed only for a fleeting moment before leaving, never to be seen until I repeated the instructions again. I didn't dislike teaching him, but he wasn't learning, and I had other things I'd rather be doing. Something had to change.

A few years ago, before starting my studio that has grown to twelve students, I had taken a pedagogy class. The professor explained the importance of connecting with the students by asking about their non-music life before beginning the lesson. He also taught that it is vital to end on a good note.

How ironic, because every lesson with Nikolai ended on a bad note.

Determined not to fail, I came up with a plan for the next lesson. We started off with a game I made up to help him understand the difference between quarter notes and eighth notes. It was similar to *Red Light, Green Light*, except that I substituted quarter notes, eighth notes, and rests instead of the lights. When I held up a notecard with an eighth note on it, Nikolai recognized it as the faster note, and raced towards the card, intent on winning the game. Laughing with glee, he captured the card and gave me a high five. I'm not sure who was more astonished when he correctly played the rhythm on the piano, him or me. Apparently games worked a lot better than I had thought; so I began to prepare more games.

As the weeks passed and I improved at making up new games, I realized it had been a good lesson if I was absolutely exhausted and Nikolai went out the door saying cheerfully, "See you next time!" Several weeks later, I suddenly noticed that Nikolai was voluntarily sitting down on the piano bench. To say I was shocked would be an understatement. Nikolai didn't stand up at all during that lesson, or the next lesson, or even the next. He also had exciting news for me; he was the only one in his music class that aced his theory test!

The long, arduous journey teaching Nikolai how to play music has helped me understand how much I love helping others. I've learned the importance of perseverance and how crucial it is to believe that a person can overcome obstacles and do a task that seems nearly impossible in the beginning. Beyond that, I've seen positive changes in all my students' attitudes and goal setting. The goals might seem unattainable at the start, but there is immense satisfaction in accomplishing them. I've learned a lot from Nikolai, but most importantly I have learned that even when confronted with a "Knick Knack Paddywack," I can face the challenge head on.

Stage Might

Anvesh J., University of Illinois at Chicago 2019

It was fifth grade and I had been asked to present my research report on the brain to my class. However, instead of actually presenting, I just stood there, mute and terrified. By the time I was eleven years old, I had developed a debilitating fear of speaking in front of almost anyone, be it a peer, adult, or complete stranger.

My fear of speaking in front of others became so bad that trying to say anything in front of an actively listening audience would leave me little more than a puddle on the floor incapable of uttering but a few syllables.

Frankly speaking, my innate shyness truly would not have been an issue under other circumstances. Many people go through life with an aversion to speaking publicly but still impact their audiences significantly. Some, Robert Frost and Richard Branson to name a few, have gone so far as to achieve widespread fame and success despite their disposition. The issue with my situation was that my interests and ambitions were not at all suited to one who was morbidly afraid of speaking.

As a child, I enjoyed taking an active role among my peers and thus applied to join the student council throughout middle school. Unfortunately, the fact that I could not speak in front of my electors made it impossible for me to be elected over other applicants, and thus I was never selected. Therefore, my discontentment with being unable to speak publicly stemmed from the fact that I had a desire to influence the world around me but an inability to do so.

The problems regarding my speaking came to a head during my eighth grade graduation, a fairly important occasion. At rehearsal the principal pronounced every name on his list and asked each of his students to correct him to avoid mispronunciation during the graduation itself. Unfortunately, when the principal butchered my last name and it was my turn to correct him, I failed to speak up, and so, in front of my family and friends, I graduated as "Anvesh Jerusalem."

Frustrated with my spinelessness, I vowed to myself the summer after eighth grade to overcome my fear of public speaking by the end of my high school career. Fueled by the embarrassment I felt at my graduation, I joined several clubs my freshman year that I would never have considered the year before, mainly the Debate Team and the Science Fair Club. Thus, I worked hard to learn to speak in front of others, but initially I struggled. To say the least, my first time competing for either club was filled with much stuttering, incoherent mumbling, and pitying looks from my audience.

Nevertheless, I refused to give up and instead chose to stay with those clubs in the hopes of eventually improving.

Now, as a high school senior, I look back and see how I've improved: I speak with confidence, not stuttering. I look people in the eye and coherently state my point. I'm certainly not the best public speaker, and I can easily list off the names of people who are better orators than I. However, what I have gained from my four years of self-improvement is a sense of self-confidence. I can now say without a doubt that, in front of others, I can convey my thoughts and feelings effectively, and I'm proud of that.

Furthermore, what was unforeseen was that this improvement would bring me more than just confidence. My participation in science fairs sparked a passion for neuroscience and a love for research into the inner-workings of the brain that had not existed previously. Thus, my quest for self-improvement has allowed me to fundamentally alter the course of my life for the better, causing changes that will impact me well into the future, not only in my choice of a career as a neurosurgeon, but also in how I interact with others.

Checkmate

Austin S., Clarkson 2017

Where the white pawns stand resolutely unstained, their shields are dark, perhaps made from the corpses of their foes. The black pawns, although actually a dark reddish brown, stand with light shields—perhaps as camouflage. If the shield is an attempt at camouflage, then it is a poor one which will not prevent the pawns from falling to protect the highborn of the back row. The astute rook stands the shortest of the privileged. He possesses the body of his allies, but the ramparts jutt out—stained with the blood of his enemies. The gallant knight, who shows nothing but loyalty to his king, suffers the bishop standing between him and his lord. The king—what majesty and prestige! His long beard shows his wisdom and his harsh eyes his rule, but the fair queen could not fail to soften his heart with her beautiful visage.

"How much?" I ask, keeping my sentences short and simple so the Russian shopkeeper could understand.

"Two thousand," she replies; however, after seeing my hesitance, she inquires, "Discount? One thousand eight hundred and seventy."

"Okay," I respond, struggling to hold in my excitement. A hand-carved chess set: my souvenir from my summer trip as a swimming delegate to the Russian Federation.

I knew how to play chess. I had been on the chess team in my elementary school, but my skills had decayed over time. I decided the only way to get a maximum return on my investment would be to learn the game again.

The next day I brought my chess set down to the lobby, eager to face an opponent. A teammate accepted my challenge. I lost. Then again. And again. And one final time before we moved on to other things. I realized just playing the game wasn't enough. I knew the basic concepts, but I didn't always understand how one move could force me to mate four turns later. As soon as I returned home, I committed to researching the game.

I found chesstactics.org and spent time practicing every day. The site presented me with a situation I would attempt to solve before studying the solution and thought process. Although I initially struggled, I improved and usually needed only one example with a new topic before I could discern it quickly myself. Whenever I got the chance, I would play against my parents or a friend. Starting out thinking only of straightforward attacks, I soon learned the different forks and skewers, forcing my opponent to net a loss four or five moves into the future. Even if I have progressed only slightly past the novice level, I have enjoyed every step.

Chess is just another way for me to satisfy my intellectual curiosity. I always seek new avenues to expand my breadth and depth of knowledge outside of the classroom, whether it be attending classical music concerts or reading books like *The Metamorphosis* and *Brave New World*. My experience and knowledge enable me to relate to a variety of people and ideas. In college my background will allow me to approach a broader context for discussions and interpersonal relationships.

Shall we play a game?

Scars and All

Haley M., Indiana University 2016

Lying in my hospital bed, with tears streaming down my face, I looked up at my mom and asked, "Am I going to die?" That was the first time I realized that maybe I was a little bit different. I had always seen myself with a scar bisecting my chest, but I had just assumed that that was normal. It wasn't until a man and a woman in white lab coats began wheeling my hospital bed down a narrow hallway that it hit me: this is not normal.

After surgery, I had numerous questions for my parents. They began explaining to me that I was born with a heart condition by the name of tetralogy of Fallot, which is the narrowing of the pulmonary valve, along with ventricular sepal defects, or hole in the heart. They discovered I had this condition sixteen hours after I was born when I turned blue in my mother's arms. After a failed shunt operation, I went through my first open heart surgery at eleven days old. Then five days before my first birthday, it was determined that I would need another open heart surgery. Luckily, I do not remember any of these surgeries, but once I reached the age of four, I became more aware of my predicament. Two days after I graduated from pre-school, the doctors replaced my pulmonary valve with one created from the sac of a cow's heart. I was angry and could not understand why all of my friends were at the pool swimming while I lay in bed with IV's in every inch of my body. I worked so hard to build up my strength to play with my friends and tried to avoid the fact that I had a heart condition. I hated that I was the only one on the soccer field who had to wear a hockey chest protector underneath her jersey, but the worst was a bone that showed through my shirts because my sternum did not grow back properly.

Once I was in seventh grade, my valve began to calcify and stop functioning. So around that Christmas, I went through my fourth open heart operation. With this surgery I began to realize that the scar was more than a line down my chest— it has made me who I am today. As I witnessed my uncle battling cancer, I began to appreciate how lucky I was to wake up in the morning and play basketball outside with my little sister. As I learned more about my condition, I began to not only accept it, but embrace it. I was no longer angry with the people who stared at my scar as I walked along the beach; instead I was proud to show off what I had overcome. I even started making jokes about it, telling people that a shark attacked me or laughing about the fact that I'm part cow. It has taken me a long time to get here, but now I commit to helping other kids with congenital heart defects. I spoke at a local high school assembly and a black tie event to help raise money for Saving Tiny Hearts charity.

With one more surgery ahead of me, I have learned to affirm who I am. And those people in white lab coats who scared me so much? Now, I aspire to be one.

Worth My Salt

Chase F., Colorado State University 2017

I tasted the pumpkin-apple salad: delicious. The caramel-apple cheesecake? Amazing. Finally, the marinated pork roast: horrifying. The first bite I took made me choke as the overwhelmingly salty pork took its toll on my taste buds.

"What happened?" I asked my sous-chef.

I could see the confusion in his eyes when he responded, "We were supposed to use a half-cup of salt, right?"

I was mortified. The centerpiece of our entire meal was potentially ruined as a result of one of my team mates using four times the required salt. I had to think quickly. The time was almost up, and as soon as the clock ran down there would be no more chances to salvage our meal.

It was the second and final day of my cooking class's "Iron Chef" competition. I loved cooking, so I was ecstatic when I was selected to be one of two executive chefs and lead one of the competing teams. As the leader of our team, I had to decide how we could save the meal. However, it wasn't the first time I needed to make a quick decision. As a basketball player, I face dozens of decision making opportunities every game; making a good pass or taking a shot could mean the difference between a championship trophy and a tiny participation ribbon. In addition to my experience in sports, I also learned adaptability and quick decision making from my job as a supervisor at a local fair. There's nothing more stressful than having to deal with irate customers and deciding whether they need a refund or another course of action.

My past experiences ultimately readied me for a quick-thinking situation in the cooking competition. I quickly grabbed the bottle of apple cider that we had used to make our caramel-apple cheesecake and doused the pork roast in cider hoping that it would balance out some of the saltiness. I grabbed a knife and a fork and tasted another bite of the roast. It tasted good, but it was all up to the judges.

This experience helped to further develop my decision making skills and my adaptability. I know in college, I'll be faced with many changes. The courses will be more challenging, and will demand more from me than I've had to give before. From roommates, to professors, to homesickness, I'll be prepared to overcome any challenge that I face.

The judges made their verdict. Pumpkin-apple salad: delicious. Caramel-apple cheesecake: amazing. Finally, the marinated pork roast: perfect.

Culture from Color

Nathaniel S., Illinois Wesleyan 2015

The tension rises as students subtly glance in my direction. Being half Haitian and half German, I'm dark enough to be mistaken as simply black and light enough for the mistake to seem clear in hindsight. The attention of the room inadvertently centers around me, which isn't unusual. To be truthful, it's been this way all week.

My sophomore English class was studying *Incidents in the Life of a Slave Girl.* The students attempted to be racially sensitive by saying "African American" instead of "black." I prefer the term "black" because I'm called "African American" when I'm not. One, I'm just American. Two, if you were to include my heritage next to "American" it wouldn't be "African," but "Haitian" or "German." I was the only black person in my class, and all eyes were on me. The obvious effort at sensitivity alleviated any hostile tension, but tension existed nonetheless.

"'We are not the creators of tension. We merely bring to the surface the hidden tension that is already alive. We bring it out in the open, where it can be seen and dealt with,'" my mother read aloud from Marin Luther King Jr.'s "Letter from Birmingham Jail." Safely in bed at seven years old I experienced my first exposure to the idea that being black would have any effect on my life.

The apprehension of being black followed me like a dark cloud, in everything from words (*dark* connotes malevolence) to life experiences. A familiarly unpleasant nervousness accompanied me when I walked into a room as the only minority.

As always, I went to books for answers. If I had experienced this feeling, others from another time must have too. I desperately wanted to understand who I was and how I came to be that way. My heritage and present condition were intricately linked, and by learning about one, I came to understand the other.

My quest continued with *The Autobiography of Malcolm X*, opposite from where it had begun. His violence and intense racial pride opposed Martin Luther King's values. His support of Garvey's separation from whites sat in my stomach like Pennzoil and I was relieved when he denounced the idea after his Islamic pilgrimage.

I continued my search in *Black Boy* and *The Bluest Eye*. Both gave me different vantage points of the single picture, which I decided meant being black stopped at your skin; any elements associated with it were purely cultural. The differences between others and myself were our experiences. With that understanding, the nervousness inside me dissolved, although the tension outside me continues.

A Blend of Opposites

Paige W., Duke University 2017

I take a deep breath as I page through my three-inch binder, letting the colored divider tabs bounce off my fingertips. Every one of my over 900 flashcards and hundreds of pages of notes has prepared me for the upcoming AP US History test. Forty-four presidents. Twelve major wars. Two hundred and thirty-six years of independence. I could easily collapse under the amount of information my brain has absorbed over the eight months leading up to this one event. But rather than drown in a tub of Ben and Jerry's Phish Food or pretend the test has disappeared, I organize. It does not matter that I must understand six inches worth of US History for my test in five days. I can conquer twenty chapters when they are properly divided.

While I place great faith in my powers of organization, I do not believe in making my bed. Just as my grandmother does not believe in texting, I do not see any value in straightening my sheets, fluffing my pillows, or arranging my comforter so that each corner is perpendicular to the corner of the bed frame. Laundry is my sworn enemy. Mountains of clean T-shirts, socks, and blue jeans grow on every bare surface in my jungle of a bedroom. When the mountains topple over, I finally succumb to the sweatshirts, yoga pants, and running shorts imploring me to return them to their proper drawer homes. Sometimes it takes a whirlpool of clothes on my floor, making the room look like the aftermath of a clothing tsunami, to convince me to surrender. How ironic that although I gain such joy from color-coding my study guides, I can rarely muster enough will to hang up a sweater. I somehow still manage to work through the towers of clothes and messy drawers. I have learned to thrive in spite of the "disaster" as my mom calls it.

My binders and my bedroom fit into opposite sides of the organization spectrum. My mirror rests in the middle. Big enough to serve as a small kitchen table, it hangs above my desk, a happy medium in my crazy world of combined chaos and order. My mirror is constantly littered with Post-it notes in hues of purple, pink, and blue—the objects I use more than my label maker and colored pens combined. Placed randomly to form perfectly proportional chaos, each square, exactly symmetrical in itself, contributes to the vibrant masterpiece. A mass of club reminders, homework due dates, and the occasional inspirational running quote form an array of importance, stringing together multiple aspects of my life in a balance of disorganized organization.

A unique mixture of contradictions, I cannot fit into one category like I often attempt to do with each history flashcard. My mirror, covered in a rainbow colored jumble of sticky slips of paper, truly reflects me. My category four hurricane of a room and organizational skills demonstrate the balance in my life, my ability to survive and thrive in all types of pandemonium, right in the middle of the rainbow spectrum. But when the mess becomes overwhelming or when a perfectly tabbed three-inch binder no longer suffices, an occasional bowl of Phish Food won't hurt.

A Symphony from Failures

Mikowai A., Northwestern University 2019

My heart raced as I walked into the blinding stage lights. I moved slowly towards the Steinway, aware of the fact that my sweaty fingers might slip on the keys while I performed.

Adjusting the bench, I glanced over to my accompanist and nodded for her to begin the opening bars.

I watched my hands fly over the keys, holding my breath through the devilish passages and making the piano sing through the lyrical parts. I became a master puppeteer, controlling all ten of my puppets with an athletic ease. I forced myself to concentrate as we approached the impressive finale. Thundering to the end, I sprang off the bench, bowing to the judges with elation.

Telling people that I play the piano is an enormous understatement. I get up early in the morning so that I can practice between five and eight hours every day. Last summer, I began learning a concerto that I wanted to perform with an orchestra. The only way to perform with an orchestra is to win a concerto competition and then be selected as the soloist. With this goal in mind, I put more time and effort into Liszt's piano concerto than I had put into any piece before. I rehearsed for months until the music had become a part of me. Finally, the day of the competition had arrived, and I had played my best.

The entire afternoon I waited with anticipation for the email that would declare that I had won the competition. That evening, I checked my email once again for what seemed like the hundredth time. But this time the announcement had arrived. I choked with shock when I read the results. I had not won first, second, or even third place! I had failed. Immediately I was filled with anguish, running up to my room to escape. What had I done wrong? Had I made some mistake? Did the judges not like me?

For the next few days, I indulged in self-pity. I enjoyed making my family feel miserable. I moped around the house, not bothering to practice, even though I had another competition the next Saturday. When I thought back to my performance, I didn't even care that I played one of the most difficult pieces written. Then I slowly began to realize that I had played a piece feared for its virtuosity and technical challenges. And I had played it beautifully. That thought seized my attention, forcing me to realize that while I had played excellently, I had in fact failed in how I handled my "failure." I viewed everything from the wrong perspective. For as long as I can remember, my dad has always told me to keep my priorities straight and to utilize whatever has been given to me. I did exactly what he warned me not to do; focus on myself and whine about how I am not good enough. Suddenly his advice that I had never quite understood completely made sense to me.

That day I made the choice to transform each failure into a success. While not achieving my goals will always disappoint me, it is from analyzing my failures that I learn most. When success comes, it is easy to brush past it, not thinking about how that success came about. Yet when failure hits, I always stop to think about what I could have done differently and how to incorporate that idea into whatever I work towards next.

Reflecting on the failures that I have learned from, I cannot help but think of each failure as a wrong note in a piece. As each failure is transformed into a success, that wrong note is wiped away, and a beautiful note replaces it. I look forward to the time when I can look back over my life and enjoy the symphony that it has composed.

Sink or Adapt

Amanda F., Loyola University Chicago 2018

One of the most underestimated, underappreciated and under-rated species in the entire world is a creature that, at first glance, seems to have been dealt the very worst hand. These creatures, axolotls, virtually blind and dull-toothed, live in a dark, desolate environment and have never evolved out of their rather unattractive, tadpole-like physique. However, after getting to know these fascinating animals, one will discover the hidden beauty in these creatures. For instance, they grew strange appendages on their faces for gills and developed lungs to anticipate major environmental changes. In addition, they have the power to regenerate certain limbs, use sensors along their bodies to find food (since their eyes are useless to their dark environment). Their eggs may even hold the key to the cure for cancer. Humans have actually been linked to these animals along the evolutionary line; however, I feel as though I am even more closely related to axolotls than others of my species, specifically for my ability to adapt to my environment, not *despite* adversity, but *because of* adversity.

I know so much about such magnificent creatures because for six months I worked at the Shedd Aquarium in Chicago. From the outset, I was a fish out of water. Coming from the well-sheltered, high-esteemed suburb of Buffalo Grove, I had no experience servicing such a diverse audience of visitors to the aquarium. Before the end of spring, I had been harassed, harangued, harried and hassled by over 50,000 strangers from around the globe. I'd been yelled at in over fifteen different languages and asked questions ("How did you get the whales out of Lake Michigan?") that made me reconsider staying long enough for my measly paycheck. I, of course, didn't really care about the money; I had been dreaming of working at the Shedd since I was a little girl. When I finally got the job, however, I realized there was more to the working world than rainbows and butterfly fish: I was now an employee. I had bosses, co-workers, responsibilities, meetings, and up to four hours of commuting back and forth via taxi, bus, water taxi, bicycle, foot, car and/or train. But I got to learn something new every day. After living in such a dark cave my whole life, I was exposed to an alien environment and developed a way of finding my way around the terrifying city. Since the city wouldn't adapt to my generally shy, nervous, unable-to-order-my-own-food-at-a-restaurant personality, I adapted to fit the city.

I learned to overcome my fear of being watched and judged. I found myself initiating conversations with Shedd visitors about their kids and vacations, and was able to sense my way around the city based on personal landmarks, like a sketchy burger place that meant I was only two blocks away from the train station. I was blind when it came to learning street signs, looking in people's eyes when I talk to them, or identifying the difference between a dogfish and a shark, but like the axolotls in the Waters of the World gallery, I adapted to not only survive, but thrive, in a potentially dangerous and curious environment. I suppose that's what motivated me to keep finding new ways to coexist with the city: the unpredictabilities. I know that college will also present its own hell or high water. Even if it involves developing a pair of gills to survive whatever life throws at me, I know that just like the axolotls, I've got to just keep swimming.

Sample School-Specific Essays

The following essays were written in response to school-specific essay prompts, including supplements to the Common Application or Coalition Application. Like the names of students featured in the Sample Personal Statements, names have been shortened and sometimes changed to protect the privacy of students sharing personal information. College graduation information (whether the student ended up attending the school he or she wrote the essay for) is provided to inspire you!

Kate Z., Vanderbilt University 2021

Prompt: Please briefly elaborate on one of your extracurricular activities or work experiences. (Vanderbilt University).

While the typical teenage girl may look forward to a lavish party or new car on her sixteenth birthday, I celebrated by finally applying for a job. My parents had always taught me to be independent, and I didn't want to rely on them to pay for everything, so I applied to Kumon, an international tutoring organization.

Twice a week after school, I head straight to work for four hours. Most students with schedules filled with AP classes and extracurriculars want to start on their homework right away, but I enjoy going to work first. At Kumon, my brain can unwind by focusing on students and parents with their own goals.

I started out as a Kumon tutor, teaching math and reading and grading student work. After a few months, though, I was promoted to the front desk, suddenly responsible for checking in with students and answering parents' questions. Working at the front desk was no doubt more intimidating at first, but I looked forward to facing the challenge. I continued to work on my communication skills, and as my manager noticed my efforts, she started training me to become her assistant. I learned how to use the Kumon system on the computer, manage the tuition payments, train new employees, and answer the phone.

I knew that I was taking on a high-pressure position, but I remembered how much I enjoyed the front desk, despite my initial stress. In the beginning, I often made mistakes, like forgetting to ask for a parent's number or typing information incorrectly into the computer. With time, I improved at my job, and my manager could rely on me to help her with the majority of the work. I knew that the company counted on me, so whether it meant working thirty minutes overtime or coming in an extra day, I never failed to do my work. I learned how to deal with the pressure, and I became more confident in taking on more challenging tasks.

Working at Kumon has taught me the importance of commitment and hard work, skills essential for my future career in the medical field. Looking back, I could not have imagined a better birthday present than procuring a job.

Caley W., Miami University 2019

Prompt: Describe your academic interests and how you plan to pursue them at USC. Please feel free to address your first- and second-choice major selections (University of Southern California).

When I was younger, one of my favorite activities was selling lemonade in front of my house. It gave me the chance to show off my business skills through marketing, customer relations, and money management. At USC's Marshall School of Business, I will be given the opportunity to strengthen my business skills.

One way the Marshall School of Business will further my growth is through its Experiential Learning Center, which gives students first-hand experience with business-like scenarios. The ELC will be of great use to me because I learn best through hands-on work, and I will be prepared to face similar scenarios in the real world.

Another way I can grow as a business student at USC is by joining one of Marshall's many student-led business organizations. By participating in these organizations, I will be able to interact with students who share my interests, receive guidance from employers and alumni, and build my networking skills.

Not only will the Marshall School of Business provide me with the opportunity to enhance my business skills on campus, but it will also offer me the global experience necessary to become an expert in the field. Through the Learning About International Commerce program, I will learn about international business and then travel abroad to meet with business leaders from around the world.

At USC, I will be given every tool I need in order to strive in the business world beyond my childhood lemonade stand.

Meghan D., University of Illinois, Urbana-Champaign 2019

Prompt: In the space available discuss the significance to you of the school or summer activity in which you have been most involved. (Georgetown)

As I sit down at the piano bench, my parents begin to shout out song requests and gather around. They sing along to Journey's "Don't Stop Believing" and smile to "Fur Elise." Whenever the music starts, so does the fun.

One would never have guessed by the noise coming from the piano that I had actually taught myself to play by ear only two and a half years ago. After a Super Bowl party filled with laughter and singing around a grand piano as "Rolling in the Deep" echoed through the house, I was determined to learn how to play. The way everyone simply connected through a song amazed me, and I wanted to be able to create that effect consistently.

Piano is important to me because it brought me into the musical community. Any time I see a piano, I sit down, and my fingers dance over the keys. I love that the piano has always been able to help me forge connections easily with those listening. When I'm at the local blood drive at the community center, I always find time to play the piano whenever there is a break without people to help. Everyone there always tells my mother afterwards how great it was to have someone "play that old thing."

So that's the beauty of spending my free time on a wooden piano bench. I get to connect with new types of people I normally wouldn't if I didn't know how to play.

Kate Z., Vanderbilt University 2021

Prompt: Explain your interest in the major you selected and describe how you have recently explored or developed this interest, inside and/or outside the classroom. You may also explain how this major relates to your future career goals. (University of Illinois, Urbana-Champaign)

Irregular Astigmatism. Those two words defined my childhood. When I was 12 years old, I was diagnosed with irregular astigmatism, which means that my vision is blurry and askew. Whenever my friends invited me to a laser tag party or asked me to play softball, I hesitated because I knew that I couldn't even pinpoint my aim. My life was not like that of a normal 12-year-old. However, my mom found an eye doctor that specialized in rare eye diseases, and he offered me a solution to correct my eyes: Atropine Sulfate. I realized that biochemistry was more than just memorizing the periodic table; biochemistry was about discovering cures. From that day on, I became fascinated with the world of biochemistry.

Intrigued by the neon pink color that resulted from mixing potassium and water and the foam that appeared from mixing hydrogen peroxide and sodium iodide, I made it a point to learn as much as I could about chemical reactions and their connection to real-world issues. During junior year, I conducted an oral presentation and wrote a research paper on the effect of hematomas on overall health. The research introduced me to a wide range of other diseases and chemical mixtures, and that was when I realized that the world of medicine is all interconnected.

I knew that I wanted a university that would offer me a solid foundation for my future in medicine as well as the opportunity to gain hands-on experience. U of I focuses on preparing students for an array of careers, which starts with providing a countless number of research opportunities. For instance, the Undergraduate Research Symposium will allow me to showcase the work I want to accomplish in college regarding current biochemical problems, such as the effect of enzymes on curing vision disorders. Not only will U of I open doors for me outside of the classroom, but its classes such as Techniques in Biochem & Biotech will prepare me for the challenges of conducting real-world research. I hope to be part of the medical innovation in the future, as I want to create medicine and launch clinical trials. U of I will guide me towards my goal, whether it be working at a pharmaceutical company or becoming a surgeon.

Special Situations: Programs and Transfers

The following essays represent a few examples of special situations, such as applying to specific programs within a school or transferring during undergraduate years.

*A.D., Northwestern University Honors Program
in Medical Education 2016*

Prompt: By applying to the GPPA programs, you are applying for a guaranteed seat in one of UICs graduate and professional programs earlier than students who apply in a traditional manner. The GPPA program seeks to understand why you have chosen your intended profession and a guaranteed path into it. What makes you an ideal candidate for guaranteed admission rather than following a traditional path to your intended profession? How would a guaranteed seat contribute to your goals as an undergraduate? (University of Illinois at Chicago GPPA Program—direct admission to medical school)

In Sanskrit, **कनधित** means *knight*, or *killer of all enemies*. While I do not foresee myself wielding a sword and battling dragons, I can picture myself donning a white coat and battling viruses and bacteria—enemies of the human body.

Coming from a family of doctors, my preliminary interest in medicine comes as no surprise. However, what really got me hooked was my experience shadowing my pediatrician, Dr. Smith. Even after thirty plus years in the field, her passion didn't wane. She would always pull me aside after a patient's visit, hand me a stack of articles, and excitedly explain the diagnosis, treatment and science behind each patient. Her passion for medicine was amazing; her passion for her patients, even greater.

One story particularly impressed me. One day, a little boy came with a slight fever and drowsiness. The mother was extremely worried, but Dr. Smith simply said it was a cold. Hours later, right before going to bed, Dr. Smith called the mother just to reassure her and check up on the little boy. On their next visit to Dr. Smith, the mother commented that she had never seen a doctor who cared so much. Watching her work and being a recipient of her care has made me realize how, as a doctor, I can be a cavalier of change: making a difference in the lives of others.

I began to volunteer at _____ Medical Center since my freshman year. My four years there have been extremely useful, highlighted by patient interaction and exposure to the hospital setting. However, the most enjoyable aspect has been discharging patients. Through the years, I have escorted a multitude of patients from their room to the front door. While patients have had different stories to tell, ranging from the perpetual losing of the Cubs to the idiosyncrasies of their children, one patient left a strong impression on me: an old drug addict who was hospitalized for kidney failure. As we waited for his car, he rattled off a long list of abused substance and pulled out a box of cigarettes. I was about to stop him before he threw the box into the nearby bushes. Seeing this made me realize the amazing ability of doctors to change a person. Like a crusader for the future, doctors were able to bring the old man back from the pits of drug abuse and send him on the trail to good health.

However, I wanted to know what medicine was like elsewhere. This past summer, I traveled to India to volunteer at Lokeswarananda Eye Foundation, a rural clinic in Purulia, India, that performs free cataract surgeries. One of the largest problems in this extremely poor area is the prevalence of cataracts; the loss of vision renders the elderly incapable of sustaining themselves. During my time at the clinic, my assignment was to seat the elderly, take their height and weight, and walk them to and from the operating room. My interaction with the patients was an extremely powerful experience. As I sat them down outside of the operating room, they all stared deep into my eyes, their gazes filled with an unforgettable fear. However, as the patients came out of the surgery, their eyes were filled with the hope that kept them alive. I saw that doctors were more than scientists of the human body: they were knights of hope.

Yet knights and crusaders are nothing without their dashing stallions. I wanted to know more about the trusty steed of medicine: research. So I became a lab intern at an HIV lab at Rush Medical Center. The lab is researching the capability of using beta-catenin, a protein, to suppress HIV replication in all cells. My goal was to find the correlation between beta-catenin and an enzyme, glutamate synthetase. The first few weeks were dedicated solely to learning about the field. I read through the enormous stack of abstracts, poring over the terminology and absorbing microbiology fundamentals. I carefully watched the researchers go through the procedure, paying close attention to the small details that could make or break the experiment. Soon enough, however, I was able to run my own trials. As I eagerly waited for PCR results or rejoiced after a successful bacterial transformation, I was hooked on research.

I know that medicine is the right career for me. I have experienced both the research and the service sides of medicine and have absolutely loved both. However, I also understand that there are a lot of sacrifices in medicine: a reality I've observed in my mother's life. I have seen her empty seats at my concerts and tennis meets. I have seen the beaten look on her face after a long day. However, I have also seen the happiness she feels when talking about her patients. I have seen the joy on her face after a delivery. I hope to gain that happiness of helping others by going into medicine, the joy of knowing that you made a difference. While it is a tough road and even tougher profession, I know that I want to become a knight of the human body.

While there are many paths to becoming a doctor, the guaranteed admission path will fit me best. Without the plethora of required classes, the time consuming applications and the stressful admissions process, I can dedicate myself to deepening my understanding of science, medicine and public health. After my time in the lab, I have looked forward to college, where the research opportunities are bountiful. The traditional path to medicine would take up a lot of time, restricting my ability to go into the lab and experience science first hand. A guaranteed seat would allow me to explore deeper into biochemistry, without the fear of not taking certain classes needed for the normal entrance.

It is this inquisitiveness and determination to learn more that makes me the ideal candidate. I am always striving to learn more and get my hands dirty. I wanted to learn more about the field of medicine, and proceeded to find a lab to research at, plan the trip to the rural eye clinic and shadow Dr. Smith on the bright and early Saturday mornings. And this thirst for knowledge is not limited to simply medicine. In the classroom, I ask question after question, hoping to understand as much as possible on that subject. When the opportunity came to establish a science club at our school, I was one of the first ones to vouch for it. Whenever there is the opportunity to take the AP class, I have chosen the AP class over the normal class. My experience with medicine, my determination and my search for more knowledge make me the ideal candidate for GPPA.

Sydney S., Boston University Honors Program 2019

Prompt: The Kilachand Honors College takes on big questions in the arts, sciences, and professions that go beyond the classroom. Write an essay of 600 words or less in response to the following issue: Which corrupts more, power or powerlessness? (Boston University Honors Program)

Neither power nor powerlessness corrupts. Rather, many humans are born with that nature already a part of their being. The possession of power or the lack of such control are states of being that provide corrupt people with the opportunity to activate their unethical tendencies. The media frequently explode with tales of shady Wall Street moguls embezzling millions of dollars, politicians at all levels taking bribes from wealthy citizens, or even a homeless man robbing a convenience store to eat for the night. Regardless of status, people often manipulate their situations to benefit personal gain with no regard to anyone else.

The world is riddled with stories of corruption. However, not every person with power uses that opportunity to take for his own benefit and leave little for those below him. Philanthropist inventors, world leaders, and business owners alike take advantage of their power differently. With his funds and intelligence, Bill Gates could easily control the majority of the planet. Instead, he chose to establish his own charitable foundation, and by 2007, he had donated over $28 billion to different charity organizations as well. Bill Gates is an example of a man who does not allow himself to be corrupted by his power.

Similarly, many powerless people approach their situations much like Gates by making positive decisions that push them toward a successful future. Over the summer, working for Public Allies, a nationwide non-profit organization, I met a girl named Kiana. Kiana is sixteen years old and cannot afford her charter school tuition but also cannot attend her dangerous public school. Instead of turning to gang violence, Kiana applied to join the Public Allies program and spend a year doing non-profit work to gain life experience and pay for her education. Kiana is an example of one "powerless" person choosing not to allow herself to give in to the common route of corruption.

The desire to possess power drives people toward success, the lack of it can push people toward desperate crime, and the possession of that control can coerce people toward dishonesty. Every person is born with the potential to take the easy route that immediately benefits himself while hurting someone else, and this evil piece of humanity originates these choices. Power does not corrupt. Powerlessness does not corrupt. Power, or the lack thereof, only acts as an instrument to drive people toward acknowledging and acting upon those tainted impulses. Power may drive society's progress, but it does not instill corruption within humans; that demoralization is waiting within from the very beginning unless a person possesses the drive to strive for a more positive approach to success.

Alli V., Notre Dame University Honors Program 2020

Prompt: How do you plan to use your four years at Notre Dame and the special opportunities offered by The Hesburgh-Yusko Scholars Program to prepare yourself to become a transformational leader? Please limit your response to 250 words or less. (Notre Dame University Honors Program)

As a future primary school teacher, I want to inspire children to do their best, infusing them with a social responsibility of understanding, compassion, and tolerance.

Notre Dame's Department of Psychology curriculum will allow me to explore child development; additionally, I will pursue a minor in Education, Schooling and Society. The research opportunities both in Psychology and ESS, including the Capstone Research seminar, will allow me to integrate both the theoretical and practical aspects of my education. This combination will provide me with the knowledge I need to persuade others of the importance of social/emotional skills in a child's development.

The Hesburgh-Yusko Scholars Program awards me the opportunity to tailor my experience to specific areas. I will become more aware with my Social Justice, Global Inquiry, and Professional Venture enrichment opportunities. As I gain a better understanding of cultures around the world, I will be able to accept the challenge of educating and inspiring children to be socially responsible.

With the knowledge I acquire from various areas of research at Notre Dame and the global enrichment opportunities with the Hesburgh-Yusko Scholars program, I will gain the tools I need to inspire others to change. The children of today are the adults of tomorrow; creating a generation of people who value social justice and kindness will impact the world in a very positive way.

Tyler A., University of Arizona 2018

Prompt: Tell us what you'd like to major in at Cornell, and why or how your past academic or work experience influenced your decision, and how transferring to Cornell would further your academic interests. (Cornell University)

His first desk was an old door on two rusty filing cabinets in the back of a friend's music shop in Atlanta. Fresh out of college with no capital, little did Steve Rosenberg, a son of two Jewish immigrants, know that he would build a company that now has its own place in the New York City skyline. I was fortunate enough to intern for his financing company, Greystone, this past summer. After this experience, I would never look at my aspirations in the same way.

I came to be inspired by that same entrepreneurial spirit that had led Mr. Rosenberg to grow his business into one of the largest privately owned government agency lending companies in the country. While maintaining a humble, driven, and honest commitment to offering the best service imaginable, he nurtured the same innovative vision that allowed him to offer new solutions to his customers.

As a young Mexican-American athlete who started off his college journey pursuing baseball, I encountered this professional experience a bit unexpectedly. When I was met with the news that my baseball career at Santa Clara University would end abruptly because of hip and back injuries, my scholarships disappearing, I was unsure if I would find a passion that satisfied my competitive spirit. I took the same traits that had led to my previous athletic accomplishments and began applying them to becoming a successful student at the University of Arizona in my home town.

Now that I have progressed on my newly found path, I can't help but recognize my growth while interning on the east coast and experiencing the innovative culture of Steve Rosenberg's company. While working on an agency lending loan origination team, I came up with an idea to automate a system that prompts new origination opportunities, allowing the current originators to work much more efficiently and productively. I am currently in the process of developing this program and look forward to seeing how it can improve Greystone's profitability.

This type of work is a career path I hope to pursue after obtaining my degree. The integration of new computer software and programs to existing business practices is going to experience significant growth in the coming future, and I want to be part of an institution that promotes this type of thinking. I believe the Dyson School of Business, which I hope to join after spending a semester majoring in Economics and Information Science at the Arts and Sciences School, fosters this type of development. The flexible curriculum within the finance concentration would invite me to explore other areas of interest and gain a broader understanding of different topics that I can apply to my core business and technology background, allowing me to better connect with businesses and their needs. By understanding a company's circumstances and vision, I can streamline the most efficient technology systems for their businesses.

I connect deeply with the Dyson School's promotion of the "go-getter," visionary frame of mind. These same qualities led Steve to birth Greystone and grow it into the national company it is today. Cornell similarly fosters a culture at the cutting edge of new ideas, setting itself apart at the forefront of the business world—exactly where I want to be.

Notes

Chapter 1

page 20   "An essay is valuable when it gives us a glimpse into the authentic personality and core of a student": Nick Spaeth, Associate Vice President for Admission, Monmouth College. Personal interview, December 7, 2016.

page 20   "Don't write about your grades": Mike Cook, Senior Associate Director of Admissions, Michigan State University. Personal interview, December 2, 2016.

page 22   ". . .college admissions can send compelling messages" (Accessed online at Harvard University, "Turning the Tide: Inspiring Concern For Others And The Common Good Through College Admissions," April 2016.) <http://mcc.gse.harvard.edu/collegeadmissions>

page 22   ". . .application essays are like student interviews": Sarah Watkins, Admissions Counselor, University of Michigan, personal interview. December 1, 2016.

Chapter 2

page 25   "We should be able to pick your essay up off the floor and know it's yours": Mary Henry, Communications Manager for Enrollment Management, Purdue University. Personal interview, November 29, 2016.

page 26   Some of the best essays "are written like a movie":

Todd Iler, Senior Assistant Director of Admissions, Purdue University. Personal interview, November 29, 2016.

page 27   "You can tell by the tone and language when students are writing trying to guess what we want to hear": Keith Gehres, Director of Outreach and Recruitment at The Ohio State University. Personal interview, November 30, 2016.

page 30   "I like the real stuff. Students shouldn't try to sound like professors": Mary Henry, Communications Manager for Enrollment Management, Purdue University. Personal interview, November 29, 2016.

Chapter 3

page 31   "I love essays that demonstrate all of the elements of good writing—clarity, organization, correct spelling and punctuation, and engaging prose": Greg Orwig, Vice President of Admissions and Financial Aid, Whitworth University. Personal interview, December 5, 2016.

Chapter 4

page 38   "Some of the most memorable topics have ranged from a guy shaving his legs to play water polo": Erin Moriarty, Director of Admissions, Loyola University. Personal interview, December 9, 2016.

page 39   Common Application Essay Prompts: (Accessed online at The Common Application, "The Common Applica-

tion Announces 2016-2017 Essay Prompts," February
2017.) <http://www.commonapp.org/whats-appen
ing/application-updates/common-application-an
nounces-2016-2017-essay-prompts>

page 40   Coalition Essay Prompts: (Accessed online at The
           Coalition for Access, Affordability & Success, "Coali-
           tion Essays," February 2016). <http://www.coalition
           forcollegeaccess.org/essays.html>

page 41   University of Michigan supplement essay prompt: (Ac-
           cessed online at University of Michigan, "University of
           Michigan Questions," February 2017.) <https://admis
           sions.umich.edu/university-michigan-questions>

page 41   Cornell University supplement essay: (Acessed online at
           Cornell University, "2017 Common Application for
           Freshman Admission: Cornell University Writing Sup-
           plement," February 2017.) <https://admissions.cor
           nell.edu/sites/admissions.cornell.edu/files/2017%20E
           ssays%20and%20Questions_0.pdf>

page 42   University of Wisconsin-Madison essay prompt:
           (Accessed online at University of Wisconsin-Madison,
           "Freshman Application Materials," February 2017.)
           <https://www.admissions.wisc.edu/apply/fresh
           man/materials.php>

page 42   University of Chicago essay prompt: (Accessed online
           at University of Chicago, "Essay Questions," February

2017.)
<https://collegeadmissions.uchicago.edu/apply/essay-questions>

page 43 "It's been years, and I still remember it. He talked about his development and growth as a cofounder of the club but told it with humor": Keith Gehres, Director of Outreach and Recruitment at The Ohio State University. Personal interview, November 30, 2016.

page 45 "He was losing his eyesight, and there was no mother in the picture": Todd Iler, Senior Assistant Director of Admissions, Purdue University. Personal interview, November 29, 2016.

Chapter 5

page 46 "Plan ahead. It's amazing how many essays are submitted in the middle of the night": Keith Gehres, Director of Outreach and Recruitment at The Ohio State University. Personal interview, November 30, 2016.

page 46 Tania Runyan, *How to Write a Poem: Based on the Billy Collins Poem "Introduction to Poetry"* (New York: T. S. Poetry Press, 2015).

page 47 "The habit of compulsive, premature editing doesn't just make writing hard. It also makes writing dead. . .": Peter Elbow, *Writing Without Teachers* (New York: Oxford UP, 1973), p. 6.

Chapter 6

page 53   "Small mistakes show you haven't done your home-
           work": Sarah Watkins, Admissions Counselor, Univer-
           sity of Michigan, personal interview. December 1,
           2016.

page 55   "Usually an essay is too long. . .The more students edit,
           the more they see parts that can be more concise and
           punchy and get to the point": Ineliz Soto-Fuller,
           Director of Undergraduate Admissions, Seattle Pacific
           University. Personal interview, December 21, 2016.

page 58   Purdue Online Writing Lab. <https://owl.english.pur
           due.edu/owl/>

Chapter 7

page 60   "This essay is your chance to show you've done the
           intellectual legwork for why you want to study your
           major and how you've explored that interest": Charles
           Murphy, Associate Director of Admissions, University
           of Illinois, Urbana-Champaign. Personal interview,
           November 28, 2016.

page 61   Northwestern University Prompt, originally accessed
           online at Northwestern University, http://admissions.
           northwestern.edu/index.html, in 2014, but no longer
           available in this version.

page 66   "Nobel Prize winners": Malcolm Gladwell, *Outliers: The Story of Success* (New York, 2008), pp. 81-83

Permissions

Also from T. S. Poetry Press

Rumors of Water: Thoughts on Creativity & Writing, by L.L. Barkat (Twice named a Best Book of 2011)

A few brave writers pull back the curtain to show us their creative process. Annie Dillard did this. So did Hemingway. Now L.L. Barkat has given us a thoroughly modern analysis of writing. Practical, yes, but also a gentle uncovering of the art of being a writer.

– Gordon Atkinson, Editor at Laity Lodge

How to Write a Poem: Based on the Billy Collins Poem "Introduction to Poetry," by Tania Runyan

How to Write a Poem uses images like the buzz, the switch, the wave—from the Billy Collins poem "Introduction to Poetry"—to guide writers into new ways of writing poems. Excellent teaching tool. Anthology and prompts included.

The Joy of Poetry: How to Keep, Save & Make Your Life With Poems, by Megan Willome

An unpretentious, funny, and poignant memoir. A defense of poetry, a response to literature that has touched her life, and a manual on how to write poetry. I loved this book. As soon as I finished, I began reading it again.

– David Lee Garrison, author of *Playing Bach in the D.C. Metro*

Field Guide Series

The Field Guide Series tutors on a practical level—
in matters of reading, writing, or the development
of writing careers.

T. S. Poetry Press titles are available online in e-book and print
editions. Print editions also available through Ingram.

tspoetry.com

Made in the USA
Middletown, DE
02 August 2018